Christ
IN THE
Psalms

AN 8-WEEK BIBLE STUDY
ON THE MESSIANIC PSALMS AND THEIR FULFILLMENT

WRITTEN BY TRACI MAE BERGEN

ISBN: 979-8-9896216-0-6

Cover and interior design by Traci Bergen
Artwork and graphics by Nicole Rethmeier

Published by Everyday Berean
www.everydayberean.com

Table of Contents

THE SCRIPTURES
- I believe the Bible is the inspired Word of God and the final authority for faith and practice. *(2 Timothy 3:16-17)*
- I believe that God used human authors under the direction of the Holy Spirit to write exactly what He wanted without error or contradiction. *(2 Peter 1:20-21)*

GOD
- I believe there is only one living and true God, an infinite Spirit, the Creator and Supreme Ruler of heaven and earth. *(Genesis 1:1, Deuteronomy 6:4, Colossians 1:16)*
- I believe that in the unity of the Godhead there are three persons: the Father, the Son, and the Holy Spirit, equal in every divine perfection, and working in distinct but harmonious roles. *(1 Corinthians 8:6, 2 Corinthians 13:14, Revelation 4:11)*

JESUS CHRIST
- I believe Jesus has always existed from the beginning with God. *(John 1:1-3)*
- I believe that the Lord Jesus Christ, the eternal Son of God, became fully human, without ceasing to be God, having been conceived by the Holy Spirit and born of the virgin Mary. *(John 1:1, 2, 14; Luke 1:35; Matt. 1:21-23)*
- I believe that Christ lived a sinless life, died on a cross, and was literally and physically raised from the dead on the third day, in order to redeem sinful mankind. *(Romans 3:24-25, Ephesians 1:7, 1 Peter 1:3-5, 1 Peter 2:24, 1 John 3:5)*
- I believe Jesus has ascended to heaven and is now exalted at the right hand of God, where as our High Priest, He acts as our Representative, Intercessor, and Advocate before the Father. *(Acts 1:9-10, Romans 8:34, Hebrews 7:25, Hebrews 9:24, I John 2:1-2)*
- I believe that the Lord Jesus Christ will return again to righteously judge the world at His second coming. *(Mark 14:24-27, Revelation 19:11-16)*

Statement of Faith

THE HOLY SPIRIT
- I believe that the Holy Spirit is a divine person, with God the Father and God the Son and of the same nature.
- I believe that the Holy Spirit convicts the world of sin, righteousness, and judgment, and that He is the supernatural agent in regeneration who baptizes all believers into the body of Christ. *(John 16:8-11, 1 Corinthians 12:13, Titus 3:5)*
- I believe that the Holy Spirit indwells every believer, sealing them for the day of redemption, and that He is their abiding Helper, Teacher, and Guide. *(John 14:26, John 16:7, Titus 3:5, Ephesians 1:13-14)*
- I believe the Holy Spirit provides spiritual gifting to each believer for the benefit of the body of Christ. *(1 Corinthians 12)*

SALVATION
- I believe salvation only occurs through faith in Jesus Christ. *(John 14:6, Acts 4:12)*
- I believe salvation is the gift of God, not gained by any righteousness of our own, but by grace through faith in Jesus Christ alone. *(Ephesians 2:8-9, Titus 3:4-7)*
- I believe all believers who have genuinely received Christ as their Savior are sealed with the Holy Spirit and are eternally secure in Christ. *(John 6:37-40, John 10:27-30, Romans 8:1, Romans 8:38-39, Ephesians 1:13-14, 1 Peter 1:5)*

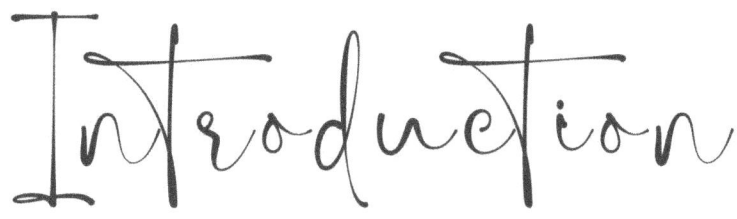

Introduction

The mission of Everyday Berean is to encourage women to know and love the Word of God in every season, and here's why this is such a burden on my heart:

I came to salvation at a young age and had read much of the Bible by the time I was an adult. When I was 20, one of my sisters invited me to attend a Bible study with her, and it was at this point that I began to realize that I didn't really know or understand what I was reading. In all of my years as a Christian, I had never learned *how* to study the Bible, and therefore came to rely too heavily on what others taught, without checking it against the truth of God's Word. When I would listen to someone teach, if something felt off, I couldn't have told you what it was. But as I learned to study the Scriptures for myself, I began to be able to discern the error of various teachers I had grown up learning from. I began to realize that many of the verses they frequently used were being taken completely out of context and didn't actually mean what I had been taught.

Through this experience I have learned how important it is for us as Christians to know God's Word for ourselves, rather than simply taking others' word for what it says. I long to be like the Bereans, who "received the word with eagerness and examined the Scriptures daily to see if these things were so," (Acts 17:11). If they, without the easy access to the Scriptures that I have, could spend time in daily study, surely I ought to have the same heart to study the Word of God with faithfulness & diligence.

With all of this in mind, I have written this Bible study with a heart to (1) give beginners some guidance as they learn to read and dig into the Scriptures for themselves and (2) give those who are more experienced something that will challenge and grow them in their ability to study well. There is minimal commentary, and I won't always provide the "right" answers to questions, because I want you to learn to think critically as you work through the text and discover its meaning on your own as much as possible.

In a culture built on ease, convenience, and immediate gratification, it is vital for us to realize that being a good student of God's Word is not meant to be a quick and easy thing to check off your list. It requires diligence, perseverance, and hard work. The ultimate goal of studying the Scriptures is not to be a "good Christian" or to get all the right answers, but to more deeply know the God who has revealed Himself through them.

In an effort to help you build your Bible study skills without "spoon-feeding" you, I have used the same set of application questions to wrap up each day's study. There are many reasons why you may be tempted to skip over these, but I encourage you to take the time to prayerfully and honestly answer these questions. This is where the real change happens: not when we simply gain knowledge of the Scriptures or even of God Himself, but when we let the Holy Spirit *use* that knowledge to make us more like Christ.

Know that I am praying for you—"that your love may abound more and more, with knowledge and all discernment, so that you may approve what is excellent, and so be pure and blameless for the day of Christ, filled with the fruit of righteousness that comes through Jesus Christ, to the glory and praise of God," (Philippians 1:9-11).

Cheering you on, friend!

Traci Mae

Founder of Everyday Berean

Week 1

CHRIST'S CHARACTER & NATURE

SCRIPTURE TO MEMORIZE: PSALM 102:26-27

they will perish
but you will remain
they will all wear out
like a garment
you will change them
like a robe &
they will pass away
but you are
the same
& your years
have no end
Psalms 102:26-27

Day 1

READ: PSALM 102

The subtitle of this psalm in the CSB reads, *A prayer of a suffering person who is weak and pours out his lament before the Lord.* The human author of this psalm is unknown; it has been attributed to Daniel, Jeremiah, Nehemiah, or other prophets who ministered during Israel's time of captivity[1]. Whoever the writer was, we see him praying in faith without sugarcoating his pain and discouragement. He knows he can safely bring his lament before God and trust Him to be strength in his weakness.

1. Read through the psalm again, noting each request the psalmist makes of God:

VERSE	REQUEST

2. Look at your list and note any synonyms or similar concepts. What do all of the requests except the last one have in common?

---

1. "Charles H. Spurgeon's Treasury of David," https://www.christianity.com/bible/commentary/charles-spurgeon/psalm/102?amp=1.

The psalmist is begging the Lord to hear him, to take notice of his suffering, and ultimately to *answer* his prayer. This should encourage us in the way we pray. We can be completely honest about our pain and discouragement when we feel like the Lord is hiding His face from us, while also full of faith in who God is and what He has said He will do.

3. What truth does the psalmist cling to in verse 17?

4. Read through the psalm again, this time taking note of words or phrases that contrast our transitory and fleeting existence with God's eternality and immutability (inability to change):

VERSE	HUMAN FRAILTY	VERSE	GOD'S ETERNALITY/IMMUTABILITY

READ: HEBREWS 1:8-12

In verses 10-12, the writer of Hebrews quotes Psalm 102:25-27, explaining that these truths are ultimately about Jesus!

5. Write Jesus' name in the blanks of Hebrews 1:10-12 below:

"_____ laid the foundation of the earth in the beginning, and the heavens are the work of _____ hands; they will perish, but _____ remain[s]; they will all wear out like a garment, like a robe _____ will roll them up, like a garment they will be changed. But _____ [is] the same, and _____ years will have no end." (Hebrews 1:10-12, ESV)

READ: JOHN 1:1-3

It may be helpful to keep your place in Hebrews 1!

6. What phrase, used multiple times in verses 1-2, is also used in Hebrews 1:10?

7. What name is used for Jesus in these first few verses of John's Gospel?

8. Look at Hebrews 1:1-2. What does it say about Jesus?

God has _____ to us by Him. (v. 2)
God _____ the world through Him. (v. 2)

9. In what ways does John reinforce the accuracy of the way the author of Hebrews applies Psalm 102:25-27 to Jesus? *(I came up with a list of six things from John 1:1-3 that line up with what Hebrews 1:1-2, 10-12 says about Jesus. See how many you can think of!)*

10. How does the author of Hebrews expand our understanding of Psalm 102:25-27?

The main goal of the writer of Hebrews is to show Jesus' supremacy. Jesus was not merely a good person or even an angel, but the eternal, unchanging God and Creator of the universe[2]! This knowledge brings such greater depth to our understanding of Psalm 102. We can apply the affliction of the psalmist to our own afflictions on behalf of Christ. When suffering and discouragement overwhelm us, we must follow the psalmist's example and pour out our lament before the Lord. Through Christ we can draw near to God's throne with confidence that we will receive mercy and grace to help in our time of need (see Hebrews 4:14-16). We know that Christ remains the same—both when He promises and when He fulfills—and therefore we as His Church have no need to fear. When we feel our human weakness and the shortness of our days, we can look to Christ who has been both our strength and our very life, and we can trust Him to continue to be such, because He is the same yesterday, today, and forever (see Hebrews 13:8).

 APPLY:

1. What did today's reading teach you about God *(any member of the Trinity)* **and His character?**

2. How do the things you've learned today change your heart?

- How do these truths shape or change your view of God?
- Has today's Scripture convicted you of any sin or wrong beliefs that you need to confess?
- Has the Holy Spirit revealed any changes that you need to make in your thoughts, beliefs, or behavior in order to walk in this truth?

---

2. See the following Scriptures for further Scriptural proof of Jesus as Creator: John 1:10; 1 Corinthians 8:6; Colossians 1:16

READ: PSALM 89

1. The psalmist declares in verses 1-2 that he will praise the steadfast love and faithfulness of the Lord. How does he immediately begin to do this in verses 3-4?

After recounting God's covenant promise to David, the psalmist goes on in verses 5-18 with more praise to the Lord for His mighty acts of faithfulness over all creation, and specifically toward His people, the nation of Israel. Then in verses 19-28, the psalmist speaks more specifically, with further remembrance of God's anointing of and covenant with David.

2. Write verse 24 below:

If you're comfortable making notes in your Bible, I suggest marking each occurrence of the words *steadfast love* and *faithfulness* in this psalm. These are clearly attributes of God that this psalmist wants to have ingrained deep in his heart.

3. Reread verses 29-37. Which two verses in this section repeat the promise stated in verse 4?

4. We know from the rest of Scripture that David's descendants broke their side of the covenant by violating God's laws. What does God promise He will do in response to their rebellion (v. 32)?

5. What is the hope given in verses 33-34 immediately following this promise of punishment?

6. According to verse 35, why can't God break His covenant with David?

God cannot go back on His word because of *who He is*. He is holy and, therefore, cannot sin against David (or anyone else) by breaking His covenant. He *must* do what He says.

READ: PSALM 132

7. In the chart below, note each request the psalmist makes of God in verses 1-10:

VERSE	REQUEST

THE LORD SWORE TO DAVID A SURE OATH
FROM WHICH HE WILL NOT TURN BACK:
"ONE OF THE SONS OF YOUR BODY
I WILL SET ON YOUR THRONE."
PSALM 132:11

8. Reread verses 11-18. The psalmist is rehearsing the Lord's promises back to Him in prayer. What promises has the Lord made concerning David, his descendants, and Zion?

VERSE	PROMISE

There are two words in verse 17 (*horn* and *lamp* in the ESV) that felt a little odd or out of place to me. I had the basic idea of what the verse was saying, but we will never regret working to gain greater understanding of God's Word! According to my commentaries, "horn" is used throughout the Old Testament to symbolize power,[1] and "lamp" symbolized life.[2]

9. Based on these definitions, rewrite verse 17 in your own words.
Don't stress about getting this answer exactly "right;" this is simply a practice to help us try to understand what we're reading!

1. John H. Walton, Victor H. Matthews, & Mark W. Chavalas, *The IVP Bible Background Commentary: Old Testament* (Downers Grove, IL: InterVarsity Press, 2000), page 514.
2. John H. Walton, Victor H. Matthews, & Mark W. Chavalas, *The IVP Bible Background Commentary: Old Testament* (Downers Grove, IL: InterVarsity Press, 2000), page 522.

READ: MATTHEW 1:1-16

10. What does this genealogy teach us about God? Consider the psalms we have just read, especially Psalm 89:29-37.

Matthew's record of Jesus' ancestors can feel boring to read, but it is a great testament to God's faithfulness! Through what appears to be a simple list of names, we can see how God remained faithful to His people for centuries. It specifically shows how He kept His promise to David that one of his descendants would be the Messiah who would reign forever!

READ: PSALM 22:9-10

We will spend week 5 digging into the rest of this psalm, so today we are only going to look at these two verses.

11. How do these verses describe Jesus? *Do your best to answer before reading on.*

These verses show us how Jesus came to earth with a job to do; He was committed to the work God had given Him *from the very beginning*. One commentary suggests that this also reflects Jesus' early consciousness that the Father's house was His true home (see Luke 2:49).[3]

READ: LUKE 1:30-33

12. Use verses 32-33 to fill in the list below.

JESUS WILL:

- _____
- _____
- _____

- _____
- _____

---

3. J.A. Motyer, *The Psalms*, ed. D. A Carson et al., *New Bible Commentary: 21st Century Edition* (Downers Grove, IL: InterVarsity Press, 2010), page 500.

This passage not only shows how Jesus was called even while still in Mary's womb, but gives us further evidence of the fulfillment of the previous two psalms we've read together today.

13. Look back at Psalm 89:4, 29, 36-37. What promises do you see repeated in Luke 1:32b-33?

After centuries of silence from God, the time had come for Him to send the promised One to redeem His people. I would love to wrap our time up today with a powerful quote from a favorite commentary:

> *"In a word, the promises had not failed but human understanding of God's time-scale and of the complexity of his world-rule was not sufficient to keep step with what he was doing. **So it is for us:** the promises never fail, though seeming delay makes some lapse into doubt (2 Pet. 3:4)—and it is not just the great promise of his coming, 'for no matter how many promises God has made, they are "Yes" in Christ.' **The promises cannot fail, though our expectations may, at any moment, be blighted. At such a time, like the psalmist, we must turn the promises into song and the disappointments into prayer.**"[4]* —*J.A. Motyer*

APPLY:

1. What did today's reading teach you about God *(any member of the Trinity)* **and His character?**

2. How do the things you've learned today change your heart?

- How do these truths shape or change your view of God?
- Has today's Scripture convicted you of any sin or wrong beliefs that you need to confess?
- Has the Holy Spirit revealed any changes that you need to make in your thoughts, beliefs, or behavior in order to walk in this truth?

---

4. J.A. Motyer, *The Psalms*, ed. D. A Carson et al., *New Bible Commentary: 21st Century Edition* (Downers Grove, IL: InterVarsity Press, 2010), page 544, emphasis added.

Day 3

READ: PSALM 2:7

Feel free to read through the entire psalm if you have time, as it will come up often throughout our study. Today's verse is kind of a peculiar one, but it speaks of Jesus as the Son of God.

1. Before we study it, what do you think this verse means?

2. Look up the word "begotten" in a dictionary and write the definition below.

When I was studying for this, I began to wonder, *What does "begotten" really mean?* After looking up the definition, I then had to ask: *How could Jesus, who is God and has always existed, be God's "begotten" Son?* Maybe you already know the answer. But if you're as confused as I was, let's dig in together.

READ: LUKE 1:31-35

3. How does verse 35 say Jesus was conceived in Mary's womb?

4. Having been conceived by God the Holy Spirit, what is this Child to be called (v. 35b)?

We do have to be careful here; it would be easy to see the word "begotten" used in reference to Jesus and claim that He couldn't be God or equal to God, because only a created being could be "begotten." What we fail to remember is that where our English Bible translations say "begotten," there was originally a Greek word: *monogenes*.

Monogenes has two primary definitions. The first pertains to being the only one of its kind within a specific relationship. This is what the writer of Hebrews means when he refers to Isaac as Abraham's "only begotten son," (Hebrews 11:17, KJV). Abraham had more than one son, but Isaac was the only one he had with Sarah, as well as the only son with which God continued His covenant relationship. The uniqueness of Isaac among the other sons makes the use of *monogenes* appropriate in that context.

The second definition pertains to being the only one of its kind or class. This is the meaning implied in the famous John 3:16 (see also John 1:14, 18; 3:18; 1 John 4:9) which calls Jesus God's "only begotten Son." John's intent was to prove that Jesus is the Son of God (see John 20:31), and he used the word *monogenes* to highlight Jesus as being *uniquely* God's Son, sharing *the same divine nature as God*, which is not true of believers who are *adopted* as God's children. In this way, Jesus is God's "one and only" Son.

It is especially important to remember that the terms we use to refer to the different members of the Trinity, such as "Father" and "Son," are human terms that serve to help us understand the relationship between them. As is true of most analogies, it breaks down if you try to take it too far and teach (as do some cults and false teachers) that Jesus was "begotten" in the sense of having been *created* by God the Father.[1] I also find it interesting to note that in newer translations (such as ESV), the word "begotten" has been removed from verses like John 3:16. I can only assume this is because it has only served to cause confusion rather than being helpful to our understanding.

READ: ACTS 13:32-33

5. According to these verses, what is the good news the apostles bring?

6. Verse 33 directly quotes Psalm 2:7. How does Luke (the writer of Acts) say God has fulfilled this and the rest of the promises He made to their ancestors?

---

1. "What Does It Mean That Jesus Is God's Only Begotten Son?" January 4, 2022, https://www.gotquestions.org/only-begotten-son.html.

7. How does Jesus' resurrection fulfill Psalm 2:7? Do your best to answer before reading on. Read Romans 1:3-4 if you need some help.

Though there had already been numerous events that served to prove His identity, the resurrection of Jesus was the most convincing piece of evidence that He was "declared to be the Son of God in power," (Romans 1:4). This decree which was declared so long before, that Jesus was God's Son, was confirmed at His resurrection.[2] It was impossible for death to hold Him because as the Son of God He has life *in His very self*!

> *"Truly, truly, I say to you, an hour is coming, and is now here, when the dead will hear the voice of the Son of God, and those who hear will live. For as the Father has life in himself, so he has granted the Son also to have life in himself." (John 5:25-26)*

8. In the first chapter of Hebrews, the writer quotes several passages of Scripture to show Jesus' superiority to angels. Look up Hebrews 1:5 and write it below, considering it in light of all that we have studied together today.

> "HE IS THE SON OF GOD, & THEREFORE OF THE SAME NATURE WITH THE FATHER, HAS IN HIM ALL THE FULNESS OF THE GODHEAD, INFINITE WISDOM, POWER, & HOLINESS."[3]
> —MATTHEW HENRY

APPLY:

1. What did today's reading teach you about God *(any member of the Trinity)* **and His character?**

2. How do the things you've learned today change your heart?

- How do these truths shape or change your view of God?
- Has today's Scripture convicted you of any sin or wrong beliefs that you need to confess?
- Has the Holy Spirit revealed any changes that you need to make in your thoughts, beliefs, or behavior in order to walk in this truth?

---

2. Matthew Henry, *Matthew Henry's Commentary on the Whole Bible* (Peabody, MA: Hendrickson Publishers, 2008), page 1696.
3. Matthew Henry, *Matthew Henry's Commentary on the Whole Bible* (Peabody, MA: Hendrickson Publishers, 2008), page 1696.

Day 4

READ: PSALM 89:26-27

1. Verse 26 is not our main focus today, but there are some great truths here about Christ that we can draw out. In the space below, write anything from this verse that you think applies to Christ:

I love what Matthew Henry says about this verse:

> *"It is probable that Solomon [cried to God as a Father]; but we are sure Christ did so, in the days of his flesh, when he offered up strong cries to God, and…taught us to address ourselves to him as our Father in heaven. … He looked upon him likewise as his God, and therefore he perfectly obeyed him, and submitted to his will in his whole undertaking…and as the rock of his salvation, who would bear him up and bear him out in his undertaking, and make him more than a conqueror, even a complete Saviour; and therefore with an undaunted resolution he endured the cross, despising the shame, for he knew he should be both justified and glorified."[1]*

2. Now for the piece we're really going to unpack—write the first half of Psalm 89:27 below:

3. Do your best to explain what you think this means in regard to Christ:

---

1. Matthew Henry, *Matthew Henry's Commentary on the Whole Bible* (Peabody, MA: Hendrickson Publishers, 2008), page 693.

READ: COLOSSIANS 1:15-20

4. Fill in the blanks below to complete all of the statements these verses make about Christ.
(I am using the ESV, but this passage is very similar in other translations.)

He is the _____ of the invisible God. (v. 15)

He is the _____ of all creation. (v. 15)

By him all things were _____. (v. 16)

All things were _____ through him and for him. (v. 16)

He is _____ all things. (v. 17)

In him _____ hold together. (v. 17)

He is the _____ of the body, the church. (v. 18)

He is the _____. (v. 18)

He is the _____ from the dead. (v. 18)

In him all the _____ of God was pleased to dwell. (v. 19)

Through him _____ are reconciled to God. (v. 20)

5. Read the passage again, this time taking note of each time the word _all_ (or a synonym, like _everything_) is used.

We're not going to spend time today digging into this particular aspect, but it is always a good practice to notice repeated words or phrases like this. It is helpful in recognizing themes, the larger purpose behind a passage, and more!

6. Jesus is called the firstborn twice in this small section of verses. Write below the two things of which He is called the firstborn:

7. What do you think verse 15 means when it calls Jesus is the firstborn of all creation? How can this be, if He is the one who created all things (v. 16)?

In our general understanding of the word *firstborn*, this could make it sound like Jesus was created—not eternal, and not God. But this disagrees with what Scripture teaches, so let's take a closer look at this passage in Colossians.

Verse 15 begins by calling Jesus "the image of the invisible God." The English word, *image*, may give us the idea of a copy that is similar but not exactly the same as the original However, the original Greek word, *eikōn*, speaks of Jesus as one who is perfectly like God the Father, revealing who He is in all His goodness, the invisible made visible. If we want to know what God is like, we can learn of Christ, because He perfectly and completely images God the Father.[2]

Colossians 1:15 goes on to call Jesus "the firstborn of all creation," which is speaking of Him not as created but as *eternal Creator*, existing before all of creation. During the time when Colossians was written, the word *firstborn* (*prōtotokos* in Greek) signified priority or rank. Therefore, calling Jesus "the firstborn of all creation" expresses His sovereign authority over it, and as we consider Psalm 89:27 ("I will make him the firstborn"), this title also recognizes Him as the Messiah.[3]

8. In Colossians 1:18, Paul also calls Jesus the firstborn from the dead. What do you think this title means?

9. Look up the following Scriptures and write down anything each passage adds to your understanding (or confusion!) of what it means for Jesus to be the firstborn from the dead:

- Revelation 1:4-6

- Acts 26:23

- 1 Corinthians 15:20-23

---

2. Peter T. O'Brien, *Colossians*, ed. D. A Carson et al., *New Bible Commentary: 21st Century Edition* (Downers Grove, IL: InterVarsity Press, 2010), page 1266.
3. "What Does It Mean That Jesus Is The "Firstborn" Over Creation?" January 4, 2022, https://www.gotquestions.org/Jesus-first-born.html.

As the first to be raised from the dead, Christ is the founder and initiator of the new life God gives believers through Jesus' victory over sin and death. His resurrection paves the way for all believers to follow Him in resurrection. So, another way to phrase this would be to say that Jesus is the firstborn of the resurrection.

There are multiple facets to this title, specifically when John uses it in Revelation, but they can be summarized in two main ideas. First, in alluding to Psalm 89:27, John shows that Jesus fulfills all history as the promised Messiah. Second, Jesus is shown to be the first to rise from the dead—the firstborn, or the beginning, of the new creation.[4]

APPLY:

1. What did today's reading teach you about God *(any member of the Trinity)* **and His character?**

2. How do the things you've learned today change your heart?

- How do these truths shape or change your view of God?
- Has today's Scripture convicted you of any sin or wrong beliefs that you need to confess?
- Has the Holy Spirit revealed any changes that you need to make in your thoughts, beliefs, or behavior in order to walk in this truth?

---

4. Justin Holcomb, "What Does It Mean That Jesus Is 'The Firstborn From The Dead'?" August 17, 2022,
https://www.christianity.com/wiki/jesus-christ/what-does-it-mean-that-jesus-is-the-firstborn-from-the-dead.html?amp=1.

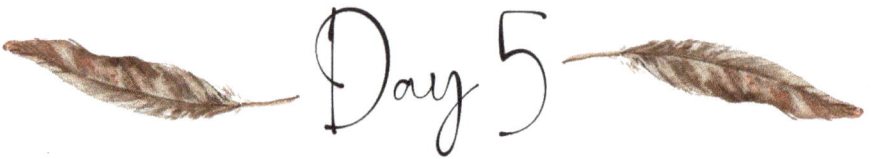

READ: PSALM 89:27

1. Finish the following sentence using the second half of Psalm 89:27:

> *"And I will make him...*

2. Look up 1 Peter 3:22. Who is this verse talking about (also read v. 21 if you're unsure), and what does it say about Him?

READ: COLOSSIANS 1:15-20

3. What four specific things does verse 16 say were created through and for Christ?

- _____
- _____
- _____
- _____

Verse 18 says that Christ is *the head of the church*, *the beginning*, and *the firstborn from the dead* so that He will be preeminent in everything. We studied the term, "firstborn from the dead," yesterday, but let's look closer at the other two.

4. Look up the following references and write down anything they add to your understanding of these truths:

- *Head of the body (the church)*: Ephesians 1:22-23

- *Beginning*: Revelation 3:14; 21:6; 22:13

5. Based on what you have just read, what does it mean that Christ is the beginning? Look up Hebrews 12:2 if you need help with your answer.

READ: REVELATION 1:5-6

6. What is the third title that verse 5 gives to Jesus?

7. Fill in the following blanks from verses 5-6 about what Christ has done for us:

"To him who _____ _____ and has _____ _____ from our sins by his blood and made us a _____, _____ to his God and Father, to him be glory and dominion forever and ever. Amen." (Revelation 1:5-6, ESV)

8. Read that last phrase again; to Christ be what two things?

I think it is common for us to hear and to say, "To God be the glory," or, "All glory to Christ," but this verse takes it a step further, not only giving Christ glory but *dominion*.

9. Look up the word *dominion* in a dictionary and write the definition that best fits the context of this passage.

23

10. Can Christ truly receive all glory without receiving all dominion? Why or why not?

When we give all glory to Christ, we are, in effect, giving Him all dominion—supreme authority and absolute ownership—over our lives. We are surrendering our own will, our own desires, and our own glory to the sovereign wisdom and will of God. In accepting Christ as Savior, we are recognizing all He has done, is doing, and will do for us, and in return we cannot help but ascribe all glory and dominion to Him for eternity! When we call Jesus our Lord we are saying that He alone is King of all and worthy of all honor and glory—preeminent in everything.

11. We'll wrap up this week by filling in the following blanks with some of the incredible titles given to Jesus:

- **Revelation 15:3b-4:**

    "Just and true are your ways, O _____ of the _____! Who will not fear, O Lord, and glorify your name? For you alone are holy. All nations will come and worship you…"

- **Revelation 17:14:**

    "They will make war on the Lamb, and the Lamb will conquer them, for he is _____ of _____ and _____ of _____, and those with him are called and chosen and faithful."

APPLY:

1. What did today's reading teach you about God *(any member of the Trinity)* **and His character?**

2. How do the things you've learned today change your heart?

- How do these truths shape or change your view of God?
- Has today's Scripture convicted you of any sin or wrong beliefs that you need to confess?
- Has the Holy Spirit revealed any changes that you need to make in your thoughts, beliefs, or behavior in order to walk in this truth?

Week 2

CHRIST'S EARLY LIFE & MINISTRY

SCRIPTURE TO MEMORIZE: PSALM 107:28

THEN
THEY CRIED
TO THE Lord
IN THEIR TROUBLE
& He delivered
them
FROM THEIR DISTRESS
PSALM 107:28

READ: PSALM 40

1. The end of verse 3 says, "Many will see and fear, and put their trust in the Lord." Look back at verses 1-2. What is it that others are seeing, causing them to put their trust in the Lord?

2. According to this psalm, what is it that brings blessing (v. 4)? How have you known this to be true in your own life?

3. In the ESV, verse 5 says, "You have multiplied, O Lord my God," while the CSB translates the same phrase as, "Lord my God, you have done many things." According to the next phrase, what is it that the Lord has multiplied, or what are the "many things" the Lord has done?

The phrasing differs between translations again, but the core idea of the second half of this verse is that the innumerable, wondrous works of the Lord should be spoken of.

4. Why is it so important that we proclaim what God has done for us?

5. Verses 9-10 give us an example of one who tells of the Lord's wondrous deeds. Using the ESV, fill in the following blanks:

> *"I have _____ the glad news of deliverance*
> *in the great congregation;*
> *behold, I have ____ _____ my lips,*
> *as you know, O Lord."*
> *(Psalm 40:9, ESV)*

"I have ____ _____ your deliverance within my heart;
I have _____ ____ your faithfulness and your salvation;
I have ____ _____ your steadfast love and your faithfulness
from the great congregation."
(Psalm 40:10, ESV)

6. Go back and circle the things the psalmist is telling of (not hiding, not concealing, etc.), **then list them out below:**

1.

2.

3.

4.

5.

6.

7. Look at the second half of verse 9. What does the psalmist say he has *not* done?

8. Now take a look at verse 11. What does he say the Lord will *not* do?

As the Lord's great mercy and love are unrestrained toward us, so our praise of the Lord should be unrestrained in response. Have you ever noticed how when you dwell on something, you begin to see reminders of it everywhere? Praise is the same. When we direct our minds to praise the Lord without restraint, we in turn will see how the Lord is unrestrained in His kindness toward us, our souls kept safe in His steadfast love and faithfulness.

9. In verse 12, what specific "evils" does the psalmist say have overtaken him?

This psalm began with the psalmist rehearsing the Lord's deliverance, and now he is asking the Lord to deliver him again—not only from suffering and persecution, but from *his own sinful heart*. He is overcome with grief over his sin and he knows the Lord is the only One who can rescue him.

WHEN WE DIRECT OUR MINDS TO PRAISE THE LORD WITHOUT RESTRAINT, WE IN TURN WILL SEE HOW THE LORD IS UNRESTRAINED IN HIS KINDNESS TOWARD US, OUR SOULS KEPT SAFE IN HIS STEADFAST LOVE & FAITHFULNESS.

10. What else does David ask of the Lord in verses 13-15? Is this a right request? Why or why not?

11. Who do we see contrasted with David's enemies in verse 16?

The contrast of these two groups of people implies that the destruction of David's enemies would in fact be just and right, because they are not seeking the Lord, and are instead opposing and harming His children.

12. David ends the psalm in verse 17 by recognizing his unworthiness, but because he knows the truth of who God is, he comes before Him with confidence that:

The Lord _____ _____ for him.
The Lord is his _____.
The Lord is his _____.

READ: LUKE 4:16-21

13. This is not a direct quotation of our psalm, but a clear *fulfillment* of it. Jesus reads Isaiah 61:1-2 in the synagogue, and what is He proclaiming? *(Refer back to Psalm 40:9 if you need a little help.)*

The "glad news of deliverance" (Psalm 40:9) is being proclaimed freely and openly. Matthew Henry says this implies that those of us called to share the gospel of Christ will be greatly tempted to hide and conceal it, because it must be shared in the face of great opposition.[1]

14. Why do you think it often feels so hard to share the gospel? How can you shift your perspective to overcome this fear?

---

1. Matthew Henry, *Matthew Henry's Commentary on the Whole Bible* (Peabody, MA: Hendrickson Publishers, 2008), page 637.

Jesus has come as the Deliverer, and *we* have been commissioned by Him to proclaim "the glad news of deliverance" to those held captive by sin! Had those who have gone before us kept this good news hidden, *we* would not have heard the gospel or tasted of the freedom we have in Christ. May we, too, boldly and publicly proclaim God's deliverance in our lives, that more captives may be set free!

1. What did today's reading teach you about God *(any member of the Trinity)* **and His character?**

2. How do the things you've learned today change your heart?

- How do these truths shape or change your view of God?
- Has today's Scripture convicted you of any sin or wrong beliefs that you need to confess?
- Has the Holy Spirit revealed any changes that you need to make in your thoughts, beliefs, or behavior in order to walk in this truth?

Day 2

READ: PSALM 69:9

Today's study is much shorter than most, so this would be a great opportunity to catch up on anything you may have skipped or to do your own research on any questions that have come up as you've studied!

We will dig into other portions of this psalm later on, so today we will only be focusing on the first half of Psalm 69:9:

"For zeal for your house has consumed me…"

1. Look at the subheading for Psalm 69 in your Bible. Who wrote this psalm?

2. We will take a closer look at verse 8 tomorrow, but these two verses are so closely connected that we really can't separate them. Based on verse 8, how was David feeling as he wrote this psalm?

3. What was specifically causing the alienation and isolation that he was experiencing (v. 9a)?

READ: JOHN 2:13-17

4. Write a brief summary of the things that happen in this passage:

5. Why is Jesus so deeply angered by the corruption happening in the temple?

The temple was supposed to be a place of worship, where people could make sacrifices and meet with God; instead it had been turned into a money-making venture. It was Christ's deep love for the Father which caused zeal for His Father's house to absolutely consume Him as He drove out those who were buying and selling. This was not an act of prideful, reactive anger, but one of self-denial, as it brought reproach upon Him from those who, in their deepest heart, held reproach for God Himself.

6. My favorite part about this short passage is that this is one of the few things Jesus didn't have to point out or explain to His disciples. What does verse 17 say the disciples did?

This is a rare occasion in which we get to see the disciples connect Jesus to a prophecy without any prompting. They were beginning to put together the pieces that would lead them to see and believe that Jesus truly was the promised Messiah, the Son of God in the flesh.

7. Are you zealous for the house of the Lord? How do you feel when you see something intended for worship being misused or abused?

APPLY:

1. What did today's reading teach you about God *(any member of the Trinity)* **and His character?**

2. How do the things you've learned today change your heart?

- How do these truths shape or change your view of God?
- Has today's Scripture convicted you of any sin or wrong beliefs that you need to confess?
- Has the Holy Spirit revealed any changes that you need to make in your thoughts, beliefs, or behavior in order to walk in this truth?

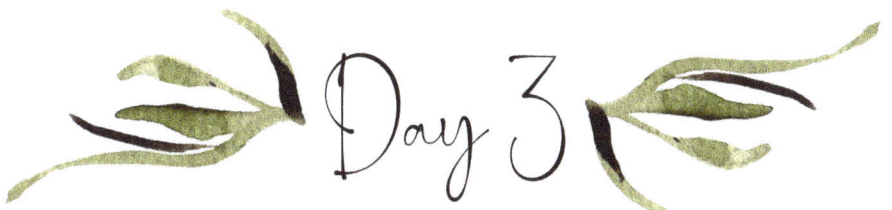

Day 3

READ: PSALM 69:6-8

1. We touched on this yesterday, but what does verse 8 say about how David was being treated?

2. What else was he receiving at the hands of those who should have been his closest allies (v. 7)?

3. What was causing this treatment? *(The first phrase in verse 7 gives us a clue.)*

READ: JOHN 1:9-12

4. What does verse 9 call Jesus?

5. Notice the repetition of the phrase, "the world," in verses 9-10. How many times does John use this phrase in these two verses?

6. In this context, does "the world" mean the earth itself or the people who live on earth?

7. Complete this list of all of the things said about the world in verses 9-10:

The _____ _____ was coming into the world. (v. 9)
He [Christ] _____ ____ the world. (v. 10)
The world was made _____ _____. (v. 10)
The world _____ _____ know Him. (v. 10)

Though Jesus is the very One who made the world, the world did not know Him. As Creator and the One in whose image they were made, He should have received the warmest, most excited welcome from the world. *Yet the world did not know Him.* They didn't recognize or even care who He truly was.

8. Who are the people that Jesus specifically came to (v. 11)?

9. Who are "his own people"? Look up Matthew 15:24 and Acts 13:45-46 if you need some help.

10. What was their response to Jesus (v. 11)?

Those who were God's chosen people, who had the very words of God which foretold the Messiah, should especially have known and received Him. Jesus Himself proved time and again during His days on earth that He was indeed the promised One, the Christ. *Yet His own people did not receive Him.*

11. In contrast to those in the previous verses, what does verse 12 say those who *do* receive Christ and believe in His name are given?

12. Look up John 5:43-47 and Acts 13:44-48. What does the Jews' rejection of Jesus as the Messiah mean for the rest of the world?

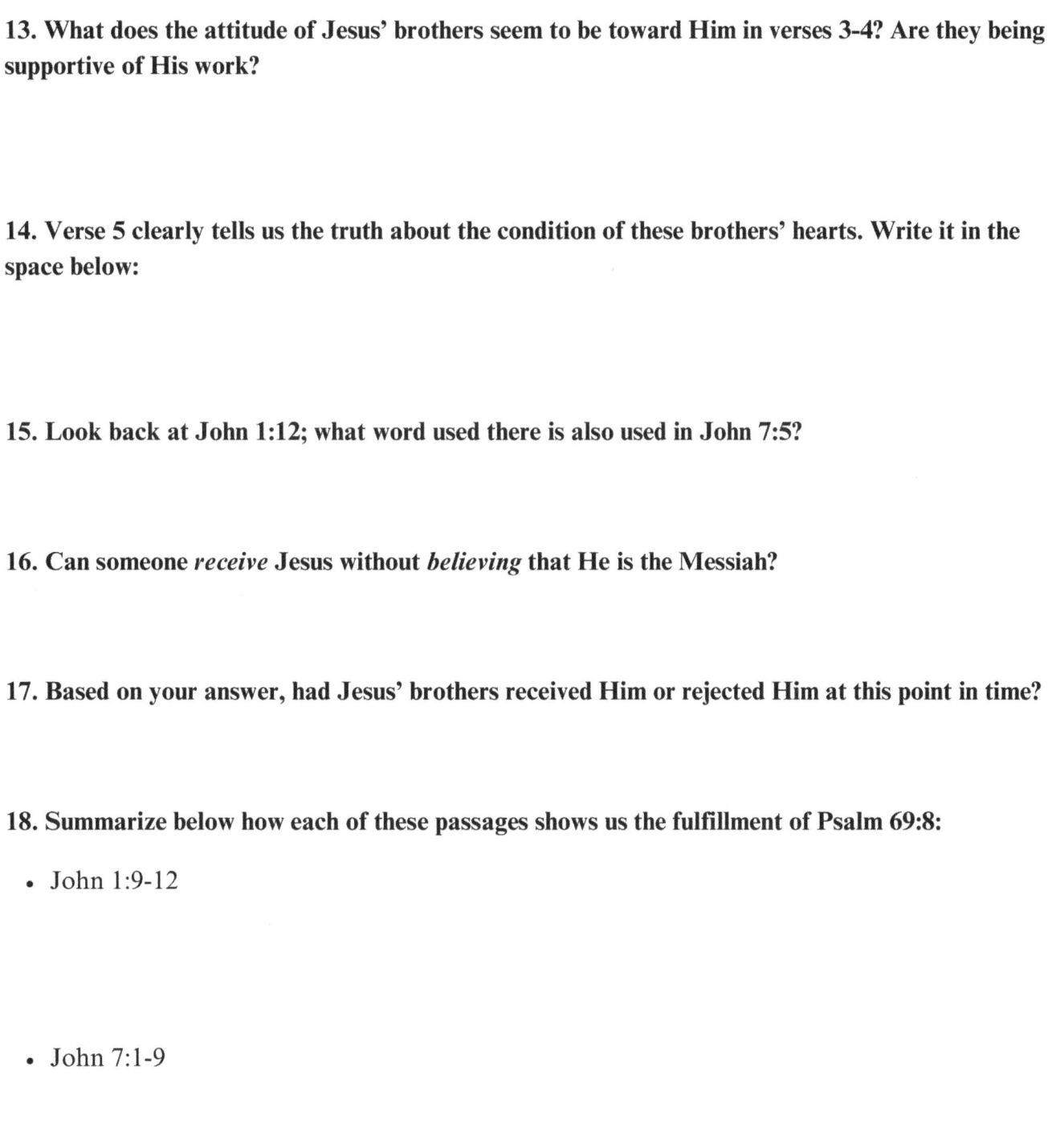

READ: JOHN 7:1-9

13. What does the attitude of Jesus' brothers seem to be toward Him in verses 3-4? Are they being supportive of His work?

14. Verse 5 clearly tells us the truth about the condition of these brothers' hearts. Write it in the space below:

15. Look back at John 1:12; what word used there is also used in John 7:5?

16. Can someone *receive* Jesus without *believing* that He is the Messiah?

17. Based on your answer, had Jesus' brothers received Him or rejected Him at this point in time?

18. Summarize below how each of these passages shows us the fulfillment of Psalm 69:8:

- John 1:9-12

- John 7:1-9

19. Have you ever experienced rejection because of the gospel? How does it comfort you to know that Christ Himself was ridiculed and rejected even by His own earthly family?

APPLY:

1. What did today's reading teach you about God *(any member of the Trinity)* and His character?

2. How do the things you've learned today change your heart?

- How do these truths shape or change your view of God?
- Has today's Scripture convicted you of any sin or wrong beliefs that you need to confess?
- Has the Holy Spirit revealed any changes that you need to make in your thoughts, beliefs, or behavior in order to walk in this truth?

WHEN WE RECEIVE CHRIST,
WE ARE ADOPTED AS GOD'S CHILDREN,
& WE CAN BE SURE THAT
HE WILL NEVER CAST US OUT!
(SEE JOHN 1:12; 6:37)

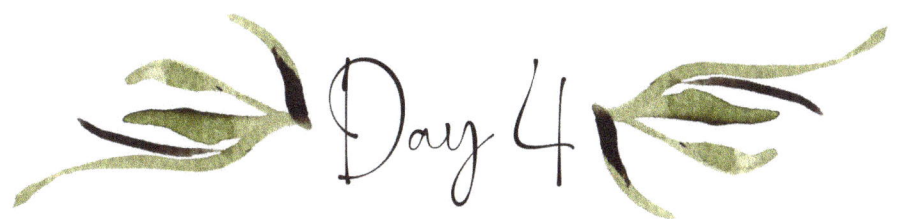

Day 4

READ: PSALM 107

1. Why does verse 1 say we are to give thanks to the Lord?

2. Skim verses 2-32 again. Which two phrases are each repeated four times?

1.

2.

3. Most of the troubles described in this psalm resulted from the Israelites' own sinful choices—direct consequences of their sin. Yet when they cried out to the Lord, how did He respond to them?

4. What do verses 2-3 call "the redeemed of the Lord" to do?

If we follow the pattern given in this psalm, our testimonies of the Lord's deliverance should not only include the more general stories of His help in our lives, but the hard stories of deliverance even from our own sin.

5. Look more closely at verses 28-29. Do they remind you of a familiar event in the New Testament?

6. Now read verses 24-25 again. Who *raised* the wind and the waves?

7. How does verse 24 describe these works of God?

8. What does this psalm repeatedly instruct us to do in regard to the Lord's wondrous works?

So then, we are called to praise the Lord for the very wind and waves that cause our courage to "melt away" (v. 26), as we recognize His sovereignty over all things and see His steadfast love even in the midst of the storm.

READ: MATTHEW 8:24-26

9. Notice how this passage begins; was it a sinful choice that put the disciples into this frightening situation?

It is important to note that the "storms" of our lives are often *not* a result of sinful or even foolish choices. Christ Himself led the disciples into the boat with Him, knowing exactly what would happen. The storm was not a consequence of sin but an avenue that Christ used to reveal Himself more fully to His disciples.

10. What is the disciples' response to their fear? How does this mirror what we have seen the people do in times of trouble throughout Psalm 107?

The sea was considered the most powerful image of uncontrolled chaos in the world during the time the Scriptures were written.[2] This would have been a significant element in the disciples' fear, and, therefore, in Jesus' act of calming the sea as well. Surely the disciples would have known this psalm, and in crying out to Jesus, they were recognizing that He had the power of

---

1. J.A. Motyer, *The Psalms*, ed. D. A Carson et al., *New Bible Commentary: 21st Century Edition* (Downers Grove, IL: InterVarsity Press, 2010), page 557.

2. John H. Walton, Victor H. Matthews, & Mark W. Chavalas, *The IVP Bible Background Commentary: Old Testament* (Downers Grove, IL: InterVarsity Press, 2000), page 551.

God Himself. "They cried to [Jesus] in their trouble, and He delivered them from their distress," making the storm be still and hushing the waves of the sea before their very eyes!

11. Based on both passages we have read today, what should our response be to each of the following circumstances?

- Trouble/distress/fear:

- Deliverance/redemption:

If that felt like a bit of a trick question, that's because it was. Prayer should be our first response in every situation, good or bad! We are always secure under the care of our Heavenly Father, but as we are battered with the storms of life, crying out to the Lord teaches us to trust His sovereignty and goodness, and to fully depend on Him in every moment. As we see His steadfast love and deliverance, we ought to burst forth in praise, thanking the Lord "for His wondrous works to the children of man!"

APPLY:

1. What did today's reading teach you about God *(any member of the Trinity)* **and His character?**

2. How do the things you've learned today change your heart?

- How do these truths shape or change your view of God?
- Has today's Scripture convicted you of any sin or wrong beliefs that you need to confess?
- Has the Holy Spirit revealed any changes that you need to make in your thoughts, beliefs, or behavior in order to walk in this truth?

THE STORM WAS NOT A CONSEQUENCE OF SIN BUT AN AVENUE THAT CHRIST USED TO REVEAL HIMSELF MORE FULLY TO HIS DISCIPLES.

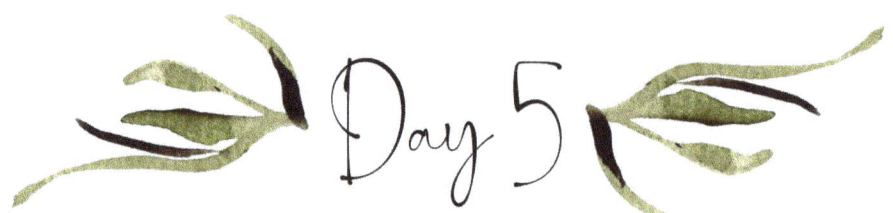

Day 5

READ: PSALM 40:6-8

We studied the rest of this psalm together earlier this week, but today we will center our focus on these three verses.

1. Verse 6 says that God has not delighted in sacrifice and offering, then takes it a step further by saying that He has not required them. We know from other parts of Scripture that He did, in fact, require and even delight in these things. What, then, do you think the writer of this psalm means by these statements?

2. Keeping your place in Psalm 40, look up Psalm 51. Read the entire psalm for context, but take special note of verses 16-17. Write down any additional insight these verses give you into the meaning of Psalm 40:6.

3. Back in Psalm 40, verses 7-8 also give us insight into the deeper meaning of verse 6. What does the psalmist say he delights in doing?

Delight in doing the Lord's will should be the heart posture of every believer! It should bring us great joy simply to obey, because the Lord has shown such steadfast love and kindness to us in all that He has done for us. The law of the Lord—His instructions to us—should be the guide that leads our hearts in the way they should go.

4. What does Jesus say He seeks in verse 30?

In verse 39 Jesus tells the people that they are diligent to search the Scriptures, which we would see as a great thing! But verse 40 tells us that, though they faithfully spent time in God's Word, they were missing the most important piece.

5. What does verse 39 say the Scriptures do?

6. Yet what are the people refusing (v. 40)?

7. Read verses 36-38 again. What/who bore witness about Jesus?

- _____

- _____

The works Jesus did while on earth, which the people saw with their own eyes, testified to the truth of His identity. Jesus also says here that God the Father has even testified about Him through His word. These people knew and based their entire lives on the Scriptures, yet they were missing the whole point! Jesus gets right to the heart of it by telling them that though they spend all this time studying and learning the Scriptures, they don't actually *believe* them—because if they did, they would believe *Him*.

8. Take another look at verse 30. How does Christ fulfill Psalm 40:8?

I DELIGHT TO DO YOUR WILL, O MY GOD:
YOUR LAW IS WITHIN MY HEART.
PSALM 40:8

9. What does verse 1 say about the original law that God gave His people?

> *"The law has but ___ _____ of the good things to come…
> it can _____, by the same sacrifices that are continually offered
> every year, _____ _____ those who draw near."*
> *(Hebrews 10:1, ESV)*

10. Can the blood of animal sacrifices cleanse people from sins (v. 4)?

11. What evidence is given to support this? *(See vv. 1b-2 if you need help.)*

12. What did Jesus say that He came to earth to do (v. 9a)?

13. By what have we who are in Christ been sanctified (v. 10)?

14. So then, what was God's will for Jesus while He lived on earth (v. 10b)?

Jesus did not come to abolish the law, but to *fulfill* it (see Matthew 5:17), in the only way that can truly take away sins. The Old Testament sacrifice of animals was a shadow, a picture of the gospel. The law opened the people's eyes to their inability to live holy lives apart from God, and gave them a vivid and continual reminder of the high cost of sin. The wages of sin is death (Romans 6:23), and *someone* has to pay that price. But praise be to God, *Someone already has*, by making the only perfect sacrifice that could ever cleanse our hearts, and He paid it once for all time!

We have of course barely scratched the surface of this passage in Hebrews, but to bring it back around to the specific fulfillment of Psalm 40:6-8, I'll leave you with this:

If we are in Christ, we can rest in the work He has done on our behalf. The wholehearted dedication to God that the psalmist spoke of has already been achieved for us by Jesus Himself, who perfectly expressed heart-level obedience and submission to God the Father throughout His earthly life. Because of this, we can take comfort in these words written by the author of Hebrews:

> *"But when Christ had offered for all time a single sacrifice for sins, he sat down at the right hand of God, waiting from that time until his enemies should be made a footstool for his feet. For by a single offering he has perfected for all time those who are being sanctified. And the Holy Spirit also bears witness to us...saying, ... 'I will remember their sins and their lawless deeds no more.' Where there is forgiveness of sins, there is no longer any offering for sin."* (Hebrews 10:12-18)

1. What did today's reading teach you about God *(any member of the Trinity)* **and His character?**

2. How do the things you've learned today change your heart?

- How do these truths shape or change your view of God?
- Has today's Scripture convicted you of any sin or wrong beliefs that you need to confess?
- Has the Holy Spirit revealed any changes that you need to make in your thoughts, beliefs, or behavior in order to walk in this truth?

Week 3

CHRIST'S LATER LIFE & MINISTRY

SCRIPTURE TO MEMORIZE: PSALM 118:22

THE STONE THAT THE BUILDERS REJECTED
HAS BECOME THE

CORNERSTONE

PSALM 118:22

Day 1

READ: PSALM 78:1-8

Feel free to read the entire psalm if you have extra time (it's fairly long). We will read an additional portion of it later, but it is always beneficial to gain the full context if you're able!

1. Who wrote this psalm?

> WE WILL NOT HIDE THEM FROM THEIR CHILDREN, BUT TELL TO THE COMING GENERATION THE GLORIOUS DEEDS OF THE LORD…
> PSALM 78:4

This psalm is ultimately about *discipleship*. It was written to remind the Israelites to tell the next generation of the works as well as the instructions of the Lord. The generation Asaph is speaking to was taught by their parents and grandparents, and now they have the weighty responsibility of passing this wisdom on to their own children and grandchildren.

2. Verse 7 reveals what should be the heart behind the sharing of God's work in our lives. Write this verse below.

3. Jumping back up to verse 2, what mode does the writer say he will use to teach the next generation?

4. What is a parable? Look it up in a dictionary if you're not sure of the definition!

A parable is often a fictitious story used for instruction. In this case, the stories used are *true* stories from Israel's past, and God, through Asaph, is using them to both instruct and warn His people.

READ: MATTHEW 13:34-35

Keep your place in Psalm 78, as we will come back to it shortly!

5. How does this passage say that Jesus taught the crowds while He was on earth?

6. Why did He teach in parables (v. 35)?

7. Look back a few verses at Matthew 13:10-17. What other reason does Jesus give for teaching in parables?

8. Was Jesus trying to conceal the truth or keep people from entering the kingdom of God?

Jesus was not attempting to keep people from God, but simply stating the fact that there are some who will never go beyond a superficial hearing of God's Word. His parables are not designed to conceal truth; rather, they fall on deaf ears because of hearts that are hardened to the truth. The ability to understand is ultimately not dependent on human ability or intelligence but is *given* by the Holy Spirit to those who are or will become true disciples of Christ.[1]

9. Think back on Psalm 78; what is the ultimate purpose behind Asaph's teaching? *(If you need a hint, look at the word in italics in the paragraph underneath question 1 of today's study.)*

10. What is the ultimate purpose behind Jesus' teaching?

---

1. R.T. France, *Reading the Gospels*, *Matthew*, ed. D. A Carson et al., *New Bible Commentary: 21st Century Edition* (Downers Grove, IL: InterVarsity Press, 2010), page 921.

11. How can you use your own testimony of God's work to encourage others to set their hope in God and walk in obedience to His Word?

READ: PSALM 78:17-32

12. What attribute(s) of God do you see displayed in this passage?

13. What phrase is repeated in verses 22 and 32?

I hope you noticed the stark contrast between God's abundant generosity, mercy, and grace, and the people's rebellion, ungratefulness, and ultimately unbelief. He was angered by their sin, and even then we see Him providing generously for their needs and working wonders on their behalf. Yet "*in spite of all this*, they still sinned; *despite his wonders*, they did not believe," (v. 32).

14. Before we move on, what specific provision is described in verses 23-25?

READ: JOHN 6:25-59

15. In verse 29, what does Jesus say is the work of God?

16. How many times does the word believe appear in this passage? Mark each occurrence if you're comfortable writing in your Bible!

17. How does this contrast with what the Israelites were doing throughout the Old Testament (reference Psalm 78:22, 32)? Whether or not they were *outwardly* following the Law, were they really doing God's work of walking in obedience?

18. What do the people ask Jesus to do in verse 30 of John 6? What do they say their response will be if He caters to their request?

19. Do you think they really would have believed had Jesus given them a sign? Why or why not?

When we consider the context of this event, especially the miracle Jesus had just recently performed in verses 1-15, we can see the shallowness of this request in verse 30. What further sign did they need than the provision of food for thousands out of minimal supplies?

20. Zooming in a little closer now, read verses 31-35 again. What does Jesus call Himself (v. 35)?

21. How does Jesus say the people have responded to Him as the Bread of Life (v. 36)?

Just like the ancient Israelites, those of Jesus' day missed the point. They wanted the Lord to provide for their *physical* needs without addressing their greater *spiritual* need. They saw God's works *with their own eyes* and did not believe. This later generation saw *Jesus Himself* and *still* did not believe. In the end, it's not so surprising that these Jews didn't understand the spiritual meaning of Jesus' words, as understanding is only possible through faith, which sadly they did not possess. If you are in Christ, spend some time today thanking Him for the gift of faith and the ability to understand the truth of His Word with the help of the Holy Spirit. These things are all too easy to take for granted, but they are no small privileges!

APPLY:

1. What did today's reading teach you about God *(any member of the Trinity)* **and His character?**

2. How do the things you've learned today change your heart?

- How do these truths shape or change your view of God?
- Has today's Scripture convicted you of any sin or wrong beliefs that you need to confess?
- Has the Holy Spirit revealed any changes that you need to make in your thoughts, beliefs, or behavior in order to walk in this truth?

Day 2

READ: PSALM 118:26-29

1. Write verse 26 in the space below:

2. What two things does verse 27 mention? Are they connected to one another? What do you think the psalmist is trying to communicate through this verse?

3. What is the light which the Lord has made to shine upon us? Look up John 1:4-5 if you need help with your answer.

4. Why would a sacrifice need to be bound to the altar?

5. How has God "made his light to shine upon us" who are on this side of the Cross?

6. Look up the following passages. Use the chart to note what each says about *light* or *sacrifice*, and anything you notice that connects the two ideas:

REFERENCE	NOTES
John 8:12	
John 12:46	
Acts 26:15-18	
Acts 26:22-23	
2 Corinthians 4:6	

I hope you were able to pick up on the fact that it is the sacrifice which brings the light! So then, as Christ allowed Himself to be fastened to the cross on our behalf—"[bound] up to the horns of the altar"—and the Holy Spirit has opened the eyes of our hearts to the gospel, we can rejoice with the psalmist that "the Lord is God, and he has made his light to shine upon us."

READ: MATTHEW 21:1-11

We won't be studying this passage in depth, but it is always helpful to gain even a small amount of understanding through simply reading the immediate context surrounding a verse.

7. Summarize the event(s) of this passage.

8. What is the general atmosphere of the streets of Jerusalem as Jesus enters?

9. Fill in the blanks from verse 9 below:

> *"And the crowds that went before him and that followed him were shouting, '_____ to the Son of David! _____ is he who comes in the _____ ____ _____ _____! _____ in the highest!'" (Matthew 21:9, ESV)*

10. What question did this great celebration leave in the minds of the people of Jerusalem, and what answer were they given (vv. 10-11)?

In these two verses, the polarization of attitudes toward Jesus becomes evident. The disciples and the Galileans recognize Jesus' allusion to the prophecy given by Zechariah (see Zechariah 9:9-10), while the residents of Jerusalem question with concern who this unknown countryman is. We will see these contrasting beliefs escalate over the next week of Jesus' life until finally those opposed to Him win out, putting Him to death.[1]

READ: PSALM 8:1-2

11. For what two things does the psalmist praise the Lord in verse 1?

12. How has the Lord established strength, according to verse 2?

13. Look up 1 Corinthians 1:26-31, and note anything below that helps your understanding of Psalm 8:2.

---

1. R.T. France, *Reading the Gospels, Matthew*, ed. D. A Carson et al., *New Bible Commentary: 21st Century Edition* (Downers Grove, IL: InterVarsity Press, 2010), page 931.

Throughout the narrative of Scripture, it is clear that God is often pleased to accomplish His great purposes through people who, in wisdom and strength, are little better than "babies and infants." Specifically in the New Testament, the apostles were looked upon as unlearned and ignorant men. Yet by the "foolishness" of their preaching, the world was turned upside down by the truth of the gospel, dealing blow after blow of defeat to the kingdom of darkness!

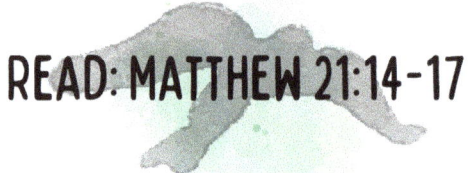

READ: MATTHEW 21:14-17

14. What did Jesus start doing when He arrived at the temple?

15. Who was crying out, "Hosanna to the Son of David!"?

16. What was significant about calling Jesus "the Son of David"?

17. Why did the religious leaders feel indignant toward Jesus (vv. 15-16)?

18. What is Jesus' response to the leaders' indignation (v. 16b)? Why is this significant?

Though the wording is slightly different from the original psalm, here we see Jesus saying that the praise of these children is a fulfillment of Psalm 8:2. In accepting their praise and especially the title they're giving Him ("Son of David"), *He is effectively declaring Himself to be the promised Messiah descended from David.*

THE CHILDREN [WERE] CRYING OUT IN THE TEMPLE, "HOSANNA TO THE SON OF DAVID!"
MATTHEW 21:15

READ: PSALM 2:6

Keep your place in Matthew 21!

19. Fill in the blanks of Psalm 2:6 below:

"As for me, I have set _____ _____
on _____, my _____ hill."

20. Where or what is Zion? *If you're not sure, just make your best guess before reading on.*

READ: JOHN 12:12-15

21. Compare Matthew 21:8 and John 12:13a. What difference do you notice in what the crowd does for Jesus?

22. Now compare Matthew 21:9 and John 12:13b. What difference do you notice in what the crowd says about Jesus?

In Scripture, Zion has two basic meanings. Literally, it was the site of the Davidic monarchy, while prophetically, it was used to refer to the center of the new creation God promised through the Messiah.[2] Both accounts quote the prophet Zechariah, who prophesied that the King of Zion would come "humble and mounted on a donkey, on a colt, the foal of a donkey," (Zechariah 9:9). Jesus' triumphal entry fulfilled a piece of the Davidic covenant and was also the beginning of the fulfillment of God's promise to make all things new!

---

2. J.A. Motyer, *The Psalms*, ed. D. A Carson et al., *New Bible Commentary: 21st Century Edition* (Downers Grove, IL: InterVarsity Press, 2010), page 489.

The waving of palm branches was a sign of honor for a conquering hero.[3] Of course Jesus was preparing to become their conquering King, but not in the way anyone thought. God's plan of redemption would have seemed foolish had anyone understood why Jesus had really come. Why *wouldn't* the Messiah come to earth as a powerful, victorious King, conquering armies and overthrowing corrupt political powers? Here is yet another example of how "the foolishness of God is wiser than men, and the weakness of God is stronger than men," (1 Corinthians 1:25). His ways are so much higher than ours! What a God we serve.

APPLY:

1. What did today's reading teach you about God *(any member of the Trinity)* **and His character?**

2. How do the things you've learned today change your heart?

- How do these truths shape or change your view of God?
- Has today's Scripture convicted you of any sin or wrong beliefs that you need to confess?
- Has the Holy Spirit revealed any changes that you need to make in your thoughts, beliefs, or behavior in order to walk in this truth?

---

3. Donald Guthrie, *Reading the Gospels, John*, ed. D. A Carson et al., *New Bible Commentary: 21st Century Edition* (Downers Grove, IL: InterVarsity Press, 2010), page 1051.

Day 3

READ: PSALM 118:22-23

1. What is the first stone mentioned in these verses?

2. What does it become?

3. Who has done this marvelous work of transformation?

4. Look up the word *cornerstone* in a dictionary and write the best definition below:

When it comes to architecture, the cornerstone is traditionally the first stone laid for a structure, and all other stones are laid in reference to it.[1] If a building is not aligned with the cornerstone, the walls, corners, and everything else will be askew.[2]

Before we jump to seeing how Christ fulfills this Scripture, I found this quote really insightful for general understanding and application concerning the rejected stone having become the cornerstone:

> *"In its original setting in the psalm this may be a proverbial saying describing a notable reversal of human opinion: who would have thought that the slave people were the chosen people, the key to human history and destiny? …who would have thought that one so humbled [referencing David] would turn out to be the acme of divine purposes?"*[3] —*J.A. Motyer*

---

1. "Architectural Cornerstones: The Meaning, History, and Intent" June 3, 2019, https://www.newstudioarchitecture.com/newstudio-blog/architectural-cornerstones.

2. Julia Prins Vanderveen, "Christ, the Cornerstone" November 4, 2018, https://todaydevotional.com/devotions/christ-the-cornerstone.

3. J.A. Motyer, *The Psalms*, ed. D. A Carson et al., *New Bible Commentary: 21st Century Edition* (Downers Grove, IL: InterVarsity Press, 2010), page 565.

Do you have any "who would have thought" circumstances in your life? I know I can think of several situations throughout my life that would never have been imagined by myself or anyone else. These things can only be attributed to being "the Lord's doing...marvelous in our eyes!" (Psalm 118:23). Praise the Lord His thoughts and ways are infinitely higher than ours (see Isaiah 55:8-9), enabling us to see His sovereign hand guiding us through *all* circumstances.

READ: MATTHEW 21:42-45

To give a little context, Jesus has just told a parable about some tenant farmers who reject their master's servants and eventually reject and even kill their master's son. (If you have time, feel free to read the parable for yourself in verses 33-41.) It is at this point that Jesus reminds the Jews of Psalm 118:22-23.

5. With this parable in mind, who have the Jews rejected throughout their history up to the time when Jesus was on earth (think back to the times of Isaiah and Jeremiah)?

6. Who were the religious leaders now rejecting?

Of this Matthew Henry says, "they would make no use of [Christ] but go on in their building without him."[4]

7. What does Jesus tell them will happen because of their rejection (v. 43a)?

8. Who does Jesus say the kingdom of God will now be given to (v. 43b)?

THE MARK OF THE NEW KINGDOM'S CITIZENS WILL NOT BE THEIR NATIONALITY, BUT THE BEARING OF FRUIT.

It is important to note here that Christ is not saying that the Jews are being replaced with Gentiles, but that God is making a new kingdom comprised of both Jews *and* Gentiles. The mark of the new kingdom's citizens will not be their nationality, but *the bearing of fruit.*

---

4. Matthew Henry, *Matthew Henry's Commentary on the Whole Bible* (Peabody, MA: Hendrickson Publishers, 2008), page 725.

READ: ACTS 4:8-12

9. Peter has been preaching the gospel and doing miraculous works, and has been arrested for it. Fill in the blanks of verse 10 below:

> *"Let it be known to all of you and to all the people of Israel that by the name of _____ _____ of Nazareth, whom _____ crucified, whom _____ raised from the dead—by _____ this man is standing before you well." (Acts 4:10, ESV)*

10. What does Peter call Jesus in verse 11?

The religious leaders would have immediately recognized this reference to Psalm 118, and many could have even been present when Jesus Himself quoted this psalm.

11. Verse 12 says there is salvation in no name other than Jesus Christ. What, then, is Peter saying the Israelites have ultimately rejected?

READ: EPHESIANS 2:19-22

12. What does Paul call believers in verse 19?

   1.

   2.

13. On what foundation is the household of God built (v. 20a)?

14. Who is the cornerstone of this foundation (v. 20b)?

15. How does this affect the whole structure, or the whole household of God (v. 21)?

16. Considering what we have learned about how cornerstones function, how must we structure our lives? Why is our foundation—our Cornerstone—so important?

WE MUST MAKE CHRIST THE FOUNDATION OF OUR HOPE, THE SOURCE OF OUR JOY, THE CENTER OF OUR UNITY, THE VERY AIM OF OUR EXISTENCE. CHRIST IS OUR LIFE (COLOSSIANS 3:4), AND AS SUCH, EVERYTHING THAT WE DO, ALL THAT WE ARE, MUST BE ORIENTED BY AND ALIGNED WITH HIM.

READ: 1 PETER 2:4-10

17. How does Peter describe Christ in verse 4?

18. What does Peter call us as believers in verse 5, and what are we being built into?

19. Verse 6 quotes Isaiah 28:16. What does it say about those who believe in the Cornerstone that God has laid in Zion?

19. What do verses 7-8 (quoting Psalm 118:22 and Isaiah 8:14, respectively) say happens to those who do not believe?

20. In contrast to unbelievers, what truths can believers hold to concerning their identity in Christ? Use verses 9-10 to fill in the following list about who we are in Christ:

A _____ race. (v. 9)

A royal _____. (v. 9)

A _____ nation. (v. 9)

A people for _____ _____ possession. (v. 9)

Made to _____ the excellencies of Christ. (v. 9)

Called out of _____. (v. 9)

Called into _____ _____ _____. (v. 9)

God's _____. (v. 10)

Given _____. (v. 10)

According to this passage, believers are the living stones of the church that Christ promised to build (see Matthew 16:18). God, our Master designer and builder, places each "stone" exactly where it will fit and function best (see 1 Corinthians 12:18). As His church we can be sure that our foundation—our Cornerstone—will never shift or crumble but will eternally support us. Because of this, we, God's holy people, are to be proclaiming His excellencies and bringing Him glory as we allow ourselves to be "built up as a spiritual house," (1 Peter 2:5), aligning our lives with Christ.

AS HIS CHURCH WE CAN BE SURE THAT
OUR FOUNDATION—OUR CORNERSTONE—
WILL NEVER SHIFT OR CRUMBLE
BUT WILL ETERNALLY SUPPORT US.

APPLY:

1. What did today's reading teach you about God *(any member of the Trinity)* **and His character?**

2. How do the things you've learned today change your heart?

- How do these truths shape or change your view of God?
- Has today's Scripture convicted you of any sin or wrong beliefs that you need to confess?
- Has the Holy Spirit revealed any changes that you need to make in your thoughts, beliefs, or behavior in order to walk in this truth?

Day 4

READ: PSALM 110

We will just be focusing on verse 1 today, but I wanted you to read the whole psalm for the sake of context, as you continue to develop good study habits.

1. Look at the heading underneath Psalm 110 in your Bible. Who wrote this psalm?

2. What invitation does God the Father extend to the Messiah in verse 1?

Even long before the His arrival, David recognized that the Messiah was not only to be a Savior but Lord and King, even called sovereign by Yahweh Himself, as He invites Him to reign with Him as King. The right hand of a king's throne is the highest honor, one of absolute power. This sitting is a resting posture, as His work was finished, but also a ruling posture, to give both law and judgment. Sitting at God's right hand denotes both the dignity and dominion of Christ, being highly honored as well as fully trusted by God the Father.[1]

3. What promise does the Father make to the Son in the second half of Psalm 110:1?

READ: MATTHEW 22:41-45

4. Who is Jesus talking to in verse 42, and what does He ask them?

---

1. Matthew Henry, *Matthew Henry's Commentary on the Whole Bible* (Peabody, MA: Hendrickson Publishers, 2008), page 717.

5. What is their response to His question (v. 42b)?

6. What is Jesus' second question to this group of Pharisees?

7. How do they respond this time (v. 46)?

8. Flip back a page or two in your Bible to Matthew 21:9, 15-16. Why did it make the religious leaders so angry when the people were calling Jesus by this name?

"Son of David" is a traditional Messianic title, and is the whole basis for the introduction of Jesus as Messiah in chapter 1 of Matthew's gospel, and Jesus Himself has already publicly accepted this title (see Matthew 21:15-16). Here in chapter 22, Jesus is not just discussing the title of the Messiah in general but *His own status* as Messiah. Jesus' point is not really to question the validity of the Messiah as a descendant of David but to show that the Messiah is *more* than that.[2] Later in Matthew, while He is on trial, Jesus uses the same description of the Son being seated at the right hand of the throne of God to claim Divine authority, and the high priest declares it blasphemy—he knows exactly what Jesus is referencing.

Jesus wanted to encourage people to think beyond earthly terms in regard to the promised Messiah. They expected a conquering hero who would be enthroned as an earthly king in Jerusalem like David[3], but God had a different plan—a better, eternal plan. The Messiah would come not as a valiant warrior but as a meek and humble servant. It was only through His rejection, suffering, and death that He would ultimately conquer evil and reign eternally as Lord of heaven and earth!

---

2. R.T. France, *Reading the Gospels, Matthew*, ed. D. A Carson et al., *New Bible Commentary: 21st Century Edition* (Downers Grove, IL: InterVarsity Press, 2010), page 933.
3. R.T. France, *Reading the Gospels, Matthew*, ed. D. A Carson et al., *New Bible Commentary: 21st Century Edition* (Downers Grove, IL: InterVarsity Press, 2010), page 934.

READ: HEBREWS 1:13-14

9. The author of Hebrews quotes Psalm 110:1 here. How does this truth prove that Jesus is superior to angels?

10. What are angels doing (v.14)?

Jesus is invited to sit at God's right hand because His work is finished (see John 19:30)! The angels are never given this privilege but are instead sent out to serve believers, both present and future ("those who *will* inherit salvation"). What a gift to us to have these servants of the Lord to accompany and protect us during our time on earth!

APPLY:

1. What did today's reading teach you about God *(any member of the Trinity)* **and His character?**

2. How do the things you've learned today change your heart?

- How do these truths shape or change your view of God?
- Has today's Scripture convicted you of any sin or wrong beliefs that you need to confess?
- Has the Holy Spirit revealed any changes that you need to make in your thoughts, beliefs, or behavior in order to walk in this truth?

Day 5

READ: PSALM 2:1-3

This psalm will lead us into the next few weeks during which we'll slowly walk through Jesus' trial and crucifixion.

1. What are the nations and peoples doing in verse 1?

2. Who does verse 2 say are counseling together in opposition to the Lord and His Anointed?

3. Who is the Lord's Anointed?

4. What is it that the kings and rulers are planning (v. 3)? What do you think this means?

The enemy loves to deceive us into thinking that the rules and restrictions the Lord has put into place are holding us back from happiness and freedom. It is an exercise in trust to believe that the commandments and statutes of the Lord have been given for our *good* (see Deuteronomy 10:12-13). But when we come to know who God is, we learn that we can trust what He says to be true and right and good, leading us to the genuine freedom and joy for which He created us.

WHEN WE COME TO KNOW WHO GOD IS, WE LEARN THAT WE CAN TRUST WHAT HE SAYS TO BE TRUE & RIGHT & GOOD, LEADING US TO THE GENUINE FREEDOM & JOY FOR WHICH HE CREATED US.

READ: MATTHEW 26:1-5

Verses 1-2 tell us that Jesus knew exactly what His future on earth held. He was not simply in the wrong place at the wrong time, a helpless victim of circumstance. Jesus' suffering was the fulfillment of God's plan of redemption, prophesied throughout Scripture long before He came to earth as a human.

5. Who does the author briefly shift attention to in verses 3-5?

In the chart below, I've compiled some historical information that will be helpful as we encounter various groups of people in our study (you may want to mark this page for easy reference):

GROUP	ROLE IN SOCIETY DURING THIS TIME PERIOD
Chief Priests	High-ranking members of the priesthood who served on the Sanhedrin (basically the supreme court of ancient Israel). They were responsible for day-to-day responsibilities at the temple.
Scribes	Learned men whose job was to study, transcribe, and write commentaries on the Mosaic Law.
Pharisees	A religious sect within Judaism, which gave oral tradition equal authority with the written Scriptures. They were more representative of the common working people and held the respect of the masses.
Sadducees	A religious sect within Judaism which was considered conservative. They did not believe in resurrection, afterlife, or spiritual beings like angels. They were typically wealthy and politically powerful.
Herodians	A political party that supported King Herod. They greatly opposed the Pharisees.

6. Where do the chief priests and elders gather (v. 3)?

7. What is the purpose of their meeting (v. 4)?

8. Look up Mark 3:6. Who is conspiring together?

9. Did the Pharisees and the Herodians work together often (see above chart)? What caused these two groups to unite during this time?

The Pharisees hated Jesus so much that they were actually willing to plot with their enemies for the sake of destroying Him. This meeting in Mark's gospel happened much earlier in Jesus' ministry than the passage we read in Matthew, but it shows us yet another fulfillment of the rulers plotting "against the Lord and against his Anointed," (Psalm 2:2).

READ: ACTS 4:1-31

10. Summarize the events of verses 1-22:

11. What do Peter, John, and their believing friends do in response to the threats they have received (v. 24)?

12. In the middle of this incredible prayer, these believers quote Psalm 2:1-2, recognizing its fulfillment in Christ's life. What purpose do they say the plotting of the rulers was ultimately accomplishing (v. 28)?

13. Because of this view of the sufferings of Jesus, this group doesn't actually pray for protection from suffering for themselves. What do they request from God instead (v. 29)?

A correct view of the sovereignty of God in suffering enabled these believers to pray not for their own comfort but for boldness to continue sharing the gospel. They fully trusted that nothing would come their way without having first passed through God's hand, and they also knew without a shadow of a doubt that without the gospel, nothing else mattered. Take note of verse 31, as God granted their request:

> "…they were all filled with the Holy Spirit and continued to speak the word of God with boldness."

14. What person do you need courage to share the gospel with today? Pray that God would grant you boldness to take the opportunities He brings!

APPLY:

1. What did today's reading teach you about God *(any member of the Trinity)* **and His character?**

2. How do the things you've learned today change your heart?

- How do these truths shape or change your view of God?
- Has today's Scripture convicted you of any sin or wrong beliefs that you need to confess?
- Has the Holy Spirit revealed any changes that you need to make in your thoughts, beliefs, or behavior in order to walk in this truth?

Week 4

CHRIST'S BETRAYAL & TRIAL

SCRIPTURE TO MEMORIZE: PSALM 109:4

I give myself to prayer

PSALM 109:4

Day 1

READ: PSALM 41:7-13

1. Who does the psalmist say is conspiring against him (v. 7, 9)?

2. David's enemies believe they have gained the upper hand. What do they say about the psalmist in verse 8?

3. What is the psalmist's response to all of these things (v. 10-13)?

READ: JOHN 13:1-30

4. What does verse 2 tell us about Judas Iscariot?

5. What does Jesus get up from the table to do for His disciples (vv. 3-5)?

6. Jesus has a short conversation with Peter in verses 6-10. What do verses 10-11 reveal that Jesus knew even before He began washing the disciples' feet?

7. Why does Jesus say His betrayal happens the way it does (v. 18)?

8. Skipping ahead to verse 26, how else does Jesus serve Judas during this meal?

We could spend an entire day studying this account and talking about what a true servant's heart looks like (and as always, feel free to wander down that rabbit trail if you have time!). But to remain focused on the fulfillment of Messianic psalms, we will be looking more specifically at the relationship between Jesus and Judas Iscariot. This account of course tells of Jesus sharing a meal with His disciples, but this would not have been the only time this happened. They would have eaten together countless times during the three years they spent together!

9. Look back at Psalm 41:9; how does it describe the one who has turned against Him?

In my experience, there is a special bond that grows between friends who share food with one another, particularly when it is a consistent pattern over the course of months or years. This also means that it brings about a special kind of hurt and devastation when those same people turn against each other. If you have experienced this kind of pain, first let me first say, I'm so sorry. It is a hard thing to suffer, and something you can't fully understand until you've experienced it firsthand. Remember that Christ Himself intimately knows the deep pain and heartache that you feel. One of His close friends decided that His very *life* was worth a few pieces of silver. And if that wasn't enough, Judas wasn't the only friend to forsake Him that night.

READ: PSALM 69:19-20

10. Take note of the repeated theme(s) in these two short verses. If you're comfortable writing in your Bible, mark the following words:
- *reproach*
- *shame*
- *dishonor*

(Other translations use slightly different words like, "insults," "scorn," or "disgrace," but for the sake of consistency I'm using the ESV unless otherwise noted.)

11. These three words (*reproach*, *shame*, and *dishonor*) **are very similar, yet distinct from one another. Look up these words in a dictionary and write their definitions below:**

WORD	DEFINITION
Reproach	
Shame	
Dishonor	

12. How does all of the shame and reproach cause the psalmist to feel? Write down as many insights as you can glean from verse 20.

READ: MATTHEW 26:36-56

Jesus takes the remaining eleven disciples to the Garden of Gethsemane, where He intends to spend time in prayer.

13. Which three disciples does He bring farther on with Him, and what does He ask them to do (vv. 37-38)?

14. What does Jesus find Peter, James, and John doing each time He returns from praying (v. 40, 43)?

15. Look back at Psalm 69:20. What similarities do you see between the psalmist and Jesus in this scenario?

16. Does Jesus run or try to hide when He notices the crowd coming to arrest Him (vv. 47-49)?

17. Does Jesus let His disciples try to defend Him against the crowd (vv. 51-53)?

18. Read verse 53 again. Do Jesus' enemies have any real power over Him?

19. What reason does Jesus give for allowing these things to happen (vv. 54-56a)?

20. How do Jesus' disciples react to all of this (v. 56b)?

Jesus looked to His close friends for support in His distress and found none, as they all fell asleep when He asked them to watch and pray with Him. In His suffering, *all* of His disciples abandoned Him and fled. He had no one left—He "looked for pity, but there was none, and for comforters, but…found none," (Psalm 69:20). When we feel betrayed, forsaken, or alone, we can follow Christ's example and lean on the strength of the Lord, "for he is the Father of mercy and the God of all comfort and consolation."[1]

21. Have you ever been betrayed or forsaken by a friend? How does it give you comfort and strength to know that Christ Himself has experienced this firsthand and understands your pain?

> "HE IS THE FATHER OF MERCY AND THE GOD OF ALL COMFORT AND CONSOLATION."
> —MATTHEW HENRY

1. Matthew Henry, *Matthew Henry's Commentary on the Whole Bible* (Peabody, MA: Hendrickson Publishers, 2008), page 669.

APPLY:

1. What did today's reading teach you about God *(any member of the Trinity)* **and His character?**

2. How do the things you've learned today change your heart?

- How do these truths shape or change your view of God?
- Has today's Scripture convicted you of any sin or wrong beliefs that you need to confess?
- Has the Holy Spirit revealed any changes that you need to make in your thoughts, beliefs, or behavior in order to walk in this truth?

READ: PSALM 35:11-16

1. Who wrote this psalm?

2. Who rises up against him (v. 11)?

3. Fill in the blanks of verse 12 below:

   "They repay me _____ for _____;
   my soul is _____."
   (Psalm 35:12, ESV)

4. What does *bereft* mean? Look it up in a dictionary if you're not sure, and write a definition below.

5. How does David describe himself as having treated these "malicious witnesses" during their time of affliction (vv. 13-14)?

6. How have they treated him in return (vv. 15-16)?

7. Before we move on, think through what you know of Jesus' earthly life. How is this—being repaid evil for good—a picture of Christ?

8. What word is used twice in verse 15?

READ: MATTHEW 26:57-63

9. What word, used twice in Psalm 35:15 (see previous question), is also used here in Matthew 26:57?

10. What attitude would the false witnesses (vv. 59-60) likely have had toward Jesus?

In this world, unfortunately people are falsely accused all the time. But no one would be more justified in defending themself than Jesus. He never sinned or did evil against anyone else. He only ever did what is *good*, and they hated Him for it, ultimately gathering together against Him "like profane mockers at a feast, [gnashing] at [Him] with their teeth," (Psalm 35:16). Yet, like the psalmist, Christ submitted all of it to the Father's good and perfect will.

11. In verse 62, the high priest demands of Jesus, "Have you no answer to make?" (v. 62). What is Jesus' response (v. 63a)?

READ: PSALM 38:13-14

Note: This psalm was written by David in response to personal sin, so the majority of the psalm is <u>not</u> messianic, as Jesus never sinned. However, the context (as always) is very helpful in understanding these two verses, so <u>I suggest giving the entire psalm a quick read-through if you have time.</u>

12. What does the psalmist mean when he says he is "like a deaf man" in verse 13?

13. What does he mean when he says he is "like a mute man" (v. 13)?

READ: MARK 15:1-5

14. Which question does Jesus answer (v. 2)?

15. What is His response to the remaining questions and accusations (vv. 3-5)?

Christ was able to "become like a man who does not hear, and in whose mouth are no rebukes," (Psalm 38:14) because He *knew* He was walking in accordance with the Father's will. We see in both Matthew's and Mark's accounts that Jesus *did* answer some of the questions He was asked during His trial. But He did *not* answer or refute any of the accusations brought against Him, instead simply choosing to remain silent. He "took no notice of the affronts put on [Him], did not resent them, nor was put into disorder by them, much less did [He] meditate revenge, or study to return the injury."[1] This was possible because He fully and confidently trusted His good heavenly Father.

16. When you are accused of something (whether true or false), is your response one of defensiveness and pride or humble trust in the One who knows all things?

---

1. Matthew Henry, *Matthew Henry's Commentary on the Whole Bible* (Peabody, MA: Hendrickson Publishers, 2008), page 634.

APPLY:

1. What did today's reading teach you about God *(any member of the Trinity)* **and His character?**

2. How do the things you've learned today change your heart?

- How do these truths shape or change your view of God?
- Has today's Scripture convicted you of any sin or wrong beliefs that you need to confess?
- Has the Holy Spirit revealed any changes that you need to make in your thoughts, beliefs, or behavior in order to walk in this truth?

Day 3

READ: PSALM 109

1. Who does the psalmist turn to in the face of wrongful accusations (v. 1)?

2. Is this the way *you* would handle a situation like this? Who is the first person you would take your problem to?

3. What type of people are speaking against the psalmist, and what kinds of things are they saying about him (v. 2-3)?

4. Skim through the entire psalm and note each occurrence of *accuse* or *accuser*. How many did you find?

In the face of slander, lies, and even assault (v. 3b), the psalmist continues to *love* his enemies (v. 4a). When we are accused, it is all too easy to react defensively! But here the psalmist's reaction to his accusers is not determined by their unjust treatment of him. Instead, he lets the commands of Scripture govern his thoughts, emotions, and actions, as he turns to the Lord in prayer.

5. How do you respond when you face accusation? How *should* you respond, based on what we have been learning this week?

THE PSALMIST'S REACTION TO HIS ACCUSERS IS NOT DETERMINED BY THEIR UNJUST TREATMENT OF HIM. INSTEAD, HE LETS THE COMMANDS OF SCRIPTURE GOVERN HIS THOUGHTS, EMOTIONS, AND ACTIONS.

READ: MARK 14:53-65

6. Who gathered together (v. 53), and what was their purpose (v. 55)?

7. Were the testimonies given during Jesus' trial legitimate (vv. 56-59)?

8. What was the only question that Jesus responded to, and what was His answer (vv. 61-62)?

9. How does this scene end? Compare verse 65 with Psalm 109:3 and make any notes or observations in the space below.

READ: PSALM 31:13-18

10. Compare Psalm 31:13a to Mark 14:56. What were both the psalmist and Christ facing in these scenarios?

11. Now compare Psalm 31:13b to Matthew 27:1. What was the goal of those plotting against the psalmist and against Jesus?

In Psalm 31, the psalmist once again responds to accusation and conspiracy with prayer and trust. Throughout the psalms we see a resistance to vengeful action, with the psalmists instead turning to the Lord in prayer, trusting *Him* to take rightful and just vengeance on the wicked in His own time. The confidence that his times were in God's hand (v. 15) enabled the psalmist to pray for deliverance from his enemies (vv. 17-18). The hand of the Lord is not the place where we are immune from life's troubles but rather the place of security in the *midst* of trouble. His hand holds us fast in trial, affliction, and suffering, even when our own grip falters.

12. Spend the remainder of your study time today meditating on Psalm 31:14-18, and use the space below to write a prayer based on these verses.

THE HAND OF THE LORD IS NOT THE PLACE WHERE WE ARE IMMUNE FROM LIFE'S TROUBLES BUT RATHER THE PLACE OF SECURITY IN THE <u>MIDST</u> OF TROUBLE.

 APPLY:

1. What did today's reading teach you about God *(any member of the Trinity)* **and His character?**

2. How do the things you've learned today change your heart?

- How do these truths shape or change your view of God?
- Has today's Scripture convicted you of any sin or wrong beliefs that you need to confess?
- Has the Holy Spirit revealed any changes that you need to make in your thoughts, beliefs, or behavior in order to walk in this truth?

Day 4

READ: PSALM 109:6-8

1. Who wrote this psalm, and what is he requesting of God in these verses?

2. Was David wrong to ask God to shorten the life of his enemy (v. 8a)? Why or why not?

Psalm 109 is what is known as an *imprecatory* psalm, meaning the author uses imprecations—curses invoking misfortune on someone—to express himself in prayer. Though we likely feel strange asking for such things with this level of honesty, it is important to remember that the psalmists wrote these not out of vindictiveness or a need for personal vengeance. Their aim was a higher, holier one. The enemies of God's people make themselves into enemies of *God*, and those who wrote this type of psalm sought vengeance on behalf of the name of the Lord, not simply their own personal hurt.[1]

As with everything, there is a balance. We should love and pray for our *human* enemies, longing for their repentance and salvation. But we must also recognize the reality of the *spiritual* enemies we face (see Ephesians 6:12)—and this often comes *at the hands of* those who are under our spiritual enemy's influence.

Specifically in Psalm 109, just before the imprecations, the psalmist affirms his love for his enemies (vv. 4-5), and the present tense indicates that his love for them *continues* throughout his interactions with them.

---

1. "What Are the Imprecatory Psalms?" January 4, 2022, https://www.gotquestions.org/imprecatory-psalms.html.

"Maybe, instead of finding here a departure from the principle of love (Mt. 5:44), we should ask whether our understanding of love is correct. Will the Lord Jesus cease to love his enemies when he subjects them to 'the wrath of the Lamb' (Rev. 6:16)?"[2] —J.A. Motyer

In the tension of the love he holds for his enemies and the hurt they are causing him, the psalmist literally says in verse 4, "But I *am* prayer." He is devoting and identifying his entire being with the posture of prayer in response to the hurt and malice he is receiving. This perfectly expresses the principle of Romans 12:19:

"Beloved, never avenge yourselves, but leave it to the wrath of God, for it is written, 'Vengeance is mine, I will repay, says the Lord.'"

3. I know this is a lot to think through; I'm leaving some space below for you to make any further notes or write down any other questions you want to research concerning imprecatory psalms.

READ: MATTHEW 27:3-5

4. What was Judas' reaction when he realized the gravity of what he had done—the verdict that Jesus would face (v. 3a)?

5. What action did Judas take to attempt to ease his guilt (v. 3b-4a)?

6. How did the chief priests and elders respond? What was their attitude toward Judas' grief?

---

2. J.A. Motyer, *The Psalms*, ed. D. A Carson et al., *New Bible Commentary: 21st Century Edition* (Downers Grove, IL: InterVarsity Press, 2010), page 559.

What happens next is hard to read, and I know suicide can be a sensitive topic. Rather than delve deeply into Judas's taking of his own life, we're going to think through *why* it happened.

7. Look up the words *remorse* and *repent* in a dictionary and compare their definitions. Was Judas *remorseful* for his actions or *repentant* of his sin? Explain your answer.

8. To whom did Judas confess his sin of betrayal (v. 4)? Was this the right avenue of confession?

9. Judas regretted his betrayal of Jesus, but there is another sin at the root of his betrayal in which Judas was deeply entangled. Read the following verses and note any insight they give you into the state of Judas's heart:

- John 12:1-6

- Matthew 26:14-16

There is not a lot of information about Judas in Scripture, but hopefully you were able to pick up on the undercurrent of the love of money in his attitude and actions.

10. Look up 1 Timothy 6:10. What does Paul say the love of money has caused in the lives of some?

11. Look up Matthew 6:24. What warning did Jesus Himself give concerning money?

This warning was given during the famous "Sermon on the Mount," which is recorded in Matthew 5-7. Judas would have been present during this time, yet it is clear that Jesus' teaching never reached his heart. In the end, rather than turning to the Lord in repentance, he turned inward, letting shame consume him. Having never tasted of God's goodness, having never experienced God's grace, Judas saw himself as irredeemable. Though he had spent three years walking side by side with God in the flesh, Judas never really came to *know* Him—how abundant His grace, how steadfast His love, how ready He is to redeem! What a true tragedy this story is.

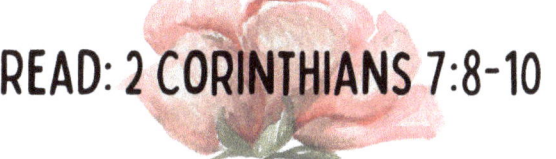

READ: 2 CORINTHIANS 7:8-10

12. What effect did Paul's first letter have on the Corinthian church (v. 8)?

13. Paul clearly states that he did not enjoy bringing grief upon the people of Corinth. What reason does he give for rejoicing in verse 9?

14. Fill in the following blanks from verse 10 to see the difference between godly grief and worldly grief:

_____ *grief produces a* _____ *that leads to* _____.
_____ *grief produces* _____.

Conviction of sin is never enjoyable, but when we consider the holiness of God and the high price that Christ paid for our sin, grief is the only appropriate response. The Holy Spirit's conviction of our sin should lead us to confess and repent, which in turn ought to produce another emotion in us.

15. Look up Luke 7:36-50. What emotion do we get to enjoy when our sins are forgiven (v. 47)?

16. Considering all that we have read and thought through today, in what way is conviction and grief over sin ultimately a gift for which we ought to give thanks?

APPLY:

1. What did today's reading teach you about God *(any member of the Trinity)* **and His character?**

2. How do the things you've learned today change your heart?

- How do these truths shape or change your view of God?
- Has today's Scripture convicted you of any sin or wrong beliefs that you need to confess?
- Has the Holy Spirit revealed any changes that you need to make in your thoughts, beliefs, or behavior in order to walk in this truth?

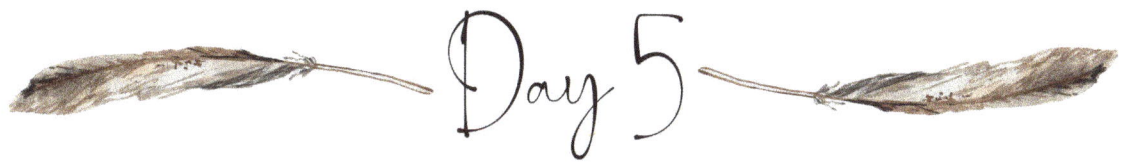

READ: PSALM 109:4-5

1. We looked at this in passing yesterday, but how did David's enemies respond to his love (v. 4a)?

2. How did they respond to the goodness David showed to them (v. 5)?

3. How did David respond to their accusations and hatred (v. 4b)?

READ: LUKE 23:32-34

4. Where is Jesus at this point, and what is being done to Him (v. 33)?

5. Fill in the blanks from verse 34:

> *"And Jesus said, 'Father, _____ them,*
> *for they _____ _____ what they do.'"*
> *(Luke 23:34, ESV)*

6. Who was Jesus praying for in this moment?

HOW INCREDIBLE IS GOD'S GRACE, THAT EVEN THE GREATEST OF SINNERS CAN REPENT & RECEIVE MERCY & FORGIVENESS.

How incredible is God's grace, that the greatest of sinners—even the very ones who condemned Christ to die—can repent and receive mercy and forgiveness. And more incredible still is that even *while* He hung on the cross, Jesus loved His persecutors and murderers enough to pray, "Father, forgive *them.*"

7. Did these people, in fact, know what they were doing? What might Christ have meant when He said, "they know not what they do"?

Matthew Henry explains it this way:

> *"The crucifiers of Christ were kept in ignorance by their rulers, and had prejudices against him instilled into them, so that in what they did against Christ and his doctrine **they thought they did God service**…This prayer of Christ was answered not long after, when many of those that had a hand in his death were converted by Peter's preaching."[1]*

8. Is there anyone you need to extend forgiveness and demonstrate love to through prayer, even if "they reward [you] evil for good" (Psalm 109:5)?

APPLY:

1. What did today's reading teach you about God *(any member of the Trinity)* **and His character?**

2. How do the things you've learned today change your heart?

- How do these truths shape or change your view of God?
- Has today's Scripture convicted you of any sin or wrong beliefs that you need to confess?
- Has the Holy Spirit revealed any changes that you need to make in your thoughts, beliefs, or behavior in order to walk in this truth?

---

1. Matthew Henry, *Matthew Henry's Commentary on the Whole Bible* (Peabody, MA: Hendrickson Publishers, 2008), page 1521, emphasis added.

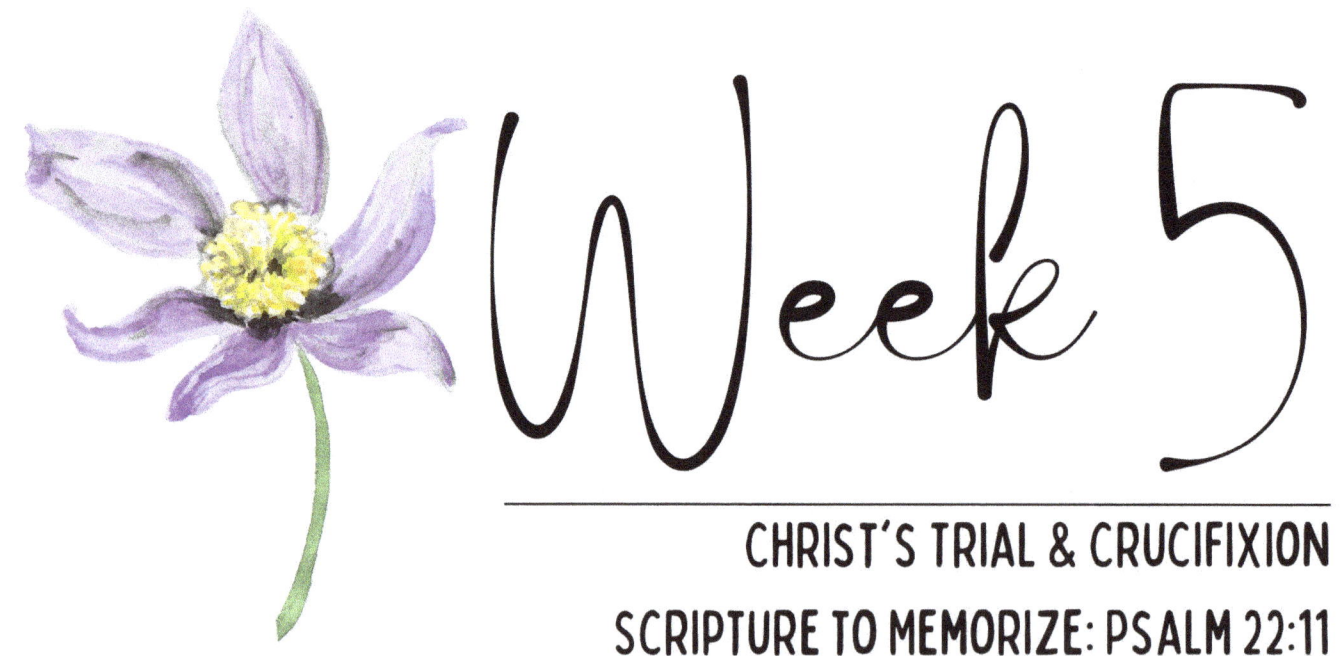

Week 5

CHRIST'S TRIAL & CRUCIFIXION

SCRIPTURE TO MEMORIZE: PSALM 22:11

BE NOT *far* FROM ME FOR TROUBLE IS *near* AND THERE IS NONE TO *help*

PSALM 22:11

Day 1

READ: PSALM 22

We will spend this entire week walking through Psalm 22. Today we will only dig into the first two verses, but be prepared to allow time to read the entire psalm as you begin your study each day.

The first two verses of this psalm are really tied together, but for our purpose of following the events of Jesus' life through the psalms, we'll begin with verse 2. The psalmist is praying "without ceasing" (1 Thessalonians 5:16), yet feeling like God isn't answering.

1. Fill in the following blanks from verse 2:

"O my God, I cry by day, but you ____ _____ _____, and by night, but I _____ ____ _____." (Psalm 22:2 ESV)

2. Have you ever fervently prayed about something, only to find that nothing seemed to change? How did that experience affect your relationship with the Lord?

READ: LUKE 22:39-46

3. What does Jesus ask of God the Father in verse 42?

> WHEN OUR PRAYERS FEEL INEFFECTIVE, WE CAN CONSIDER JESUS.

4. What is the posture of Jesus' heart as He makes His request (v. 42b)?

5. How does verse 44 tell us Jesus was feeling during this time?

6. Though Jesus prayed so earnestly that "his sweat became like great drops of blood falling down," (v. 44), God did not grant His request. What did Jesus receive as a result of His prayers (v. 43)?

Jesus knew the Father's will, and knew exactly what His future held. Yet in His distress He cried out to God the Father three different times (see parallel passage Matthew 26:36-44), each time in absolute agony yet complete surrender. When our prayers feel ineffective, we can consider Jesus. Even as He prayed, He knew that God would say "no" to His request, but He also knew that in His humanity He needed the strength prayer provides—and we need it even more so. We "ought always to pray and not lose heart," (Luke 18:1), because prayer gives us the strength to keep going, *even when our circumstances don't change.*

"This is holy ground. We have here a privileged glimpse into Jesus' intimate relation with his Father and a sobering insight into the cost of his mission."[1] —R.T. France

7. Turn back to Psalm 22 and fill in the blanks from verse 1 below:

> *"My God, my God, why have you _____ me?*
> *Why are you ____ _____ from saving me, from the _____ of my*
> *_____?" (Psalm 22:1 ESV)*

PRAYER GIVES US THE STRENGTH TO KEEP GOING, EVEN WHEN OUR CIRCUMSTANCES DON'T CHANGE.

---

1. R.T. France, *Reading the Gospels, Matthew*, ed. D. A Carson et al., *New Bible Commentary: 21st Century Edition* (Downers Grove, IL: InterVarsity Press, 2010), page 940.

READ: MATTHEW 27:45-46

8. What does verse 45 tell us happened between "the sixth hour" (noon) and "the ninth hour" (3:00 p.m.)? What do you think it signified?

9. What did Jesus cry out after these three hours of darkness, and what does it mean (v. 46)?

10. Hopefully you recognized this quote from Psalm 22:1. How can we follow Christ's example of using the Scriptures to interpret and guide our emotions? Why is this important?

11. What is the significance of God the Father having forsaken God the Son while He hung on the cross? Look up 2 Corinthians 5:21 to help with your answer.

The supernatural darkness during Christ's crucifixion is believed to be a picture of God's wrath, and not only toward those who had rejected His Son. The wrath of our holy God was directed at Jesus Himself, as He bore our sins as the perfect sacrificial Lamb.[2] It is interesting to note that this was the only time Jesus did not address God as "Father," giving further indication that the intimate relationship they enjoyed had been broken.[3] As a member of the Trinity, God the

---

2. Alan Cole, *Reading the Gospels, Mark*, ed. D. A Carson et al., *New Bible Commentary: 21st Century Edition* (Downers Grove, IL: InterVarsity Press, 2010), page 975.

3. R.T. France, *Reading the Gospels, Matthew*, ed. D. A Carson et al., *New Bible Commentary: 21st Century Edition* (Downers Grove, IL: InterVarsity Press, 2010), page 943.

Son enjoyed perfect community with God the Father and God the Holy Spirit, dwelling eternally in perfect unity with one another. Yet as He hung on the cross, Jesus felt the actual *lack* of His Father's presence for the first—and last—time. God the Father turned His face away as Christ became sin for us, bearing God's holy wrath so that *we* may become righteous (see 2 Corinthians 5:21). Jesus was forsaken by God so that we would never have to be.

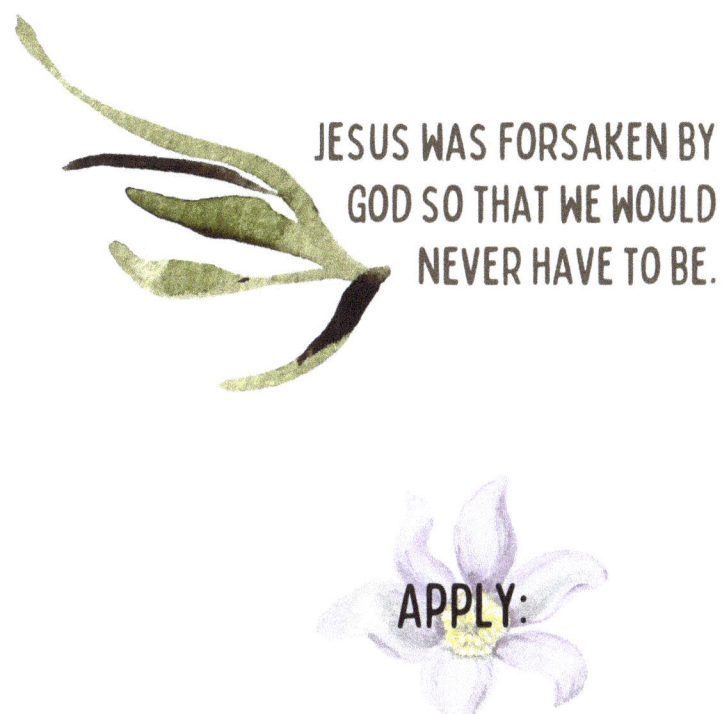

JESUS WAS FORSAKEN BY GOD SO THAT WE WOULD NEVER HAVE TO BE.

APPLY:

1. What did today's reading teach you about God *(any member of the Trinity)* **and His character?**

2. How do the things you've learned today change your heart?

- How do these truths shape or change your view of God?
- Has today's Scripture convicted you of any sin or wrong beliefs that you need to confess?
- Has the Holy Spirit revealed any changes that you need to make in your thoughts, beliefs, or behavior in order to walk in this truth?

READ: PSALM 22

1. What does the psalmist call himself at the beginning of verse 6? What do you think he means by this?

2. Look up the following passages, noticing especially the figurative use of the term "worm." Use the space below to note anything that helps you understand how this metaphor is typically used in the Bible.

- Job 25:4-6

- Isaiah 41:13-14

3. How does the psalmist say others are treating him (vv. 6-7)?

4. Who, specifically, is treating him this way (three different groups are named):

5. Verse 7 uses a phrase that is unfamiliar to us today; what do you think the psalmist means when he says, "they make mouths at me"?

6. Fill in the following blanks from verse 8:

"He _____ in _____ _____; let him _____ him;
let him _____ him, for he _____ in him!"
(Psalm 22:8 ESV)

READ: LUKE 23:13-25

7. What three groups does Pilate assemble (v. 13)?

8. Does one of these groups sound familiar? *Look back at Psalm 22:6 if you can't remember!*

Throughout the Bible, this phrase—"the people"—is typically used to refer specifically to the Israelites. They are the ones God chose to be His people and who for hundreds of years looked forward to the promised Messiah.

9. Read Luke 23:13-25 again and note below how Jesus is treated by each people group in this passage:

- Israelites

- Gentiles (Pilate and Herod)

10. In what way(s) does this fulfill Psalm 22:6?

READ: MATTHEW 27:39-44

11. Which verse specifically fulfills Psalm 22:7? Describe what happens.

12. How did those who mocked Jesus want Him to prove His deity and power (vv. 40-42)?

13. Jesus of course had the power to come down from the cross and save Himself; why did He choose not to? Why wouldn't He cater to their requests to prove who He was?

One commentary suggests that the very act of staying on the cross is what proved Christ to be the Son of God.[1] It wasn't the nails that held Jesus on the cross, but His steadfast love for humanity combined with His perfect obedience to the will of the Father. Those who mocked Him assumed that He *could* not save Himself and therefore had been lying about His identity and power. The reality was that He *would* not save Himself, because He knew He must die to save *us*.

> IT WASN'T THE NAILS THAT HELD JESUS ON THE CROSS, BUT HIS STEADFAST LOVE FOR HUMANITY COMBINED WITH HIS PERFECT OBEDIENCE TO THE WILL OF THE FATHER.

14. Verse 43 closely resembles Psalm 22:8. What aspect of Christ's character is being mocked here?

---

1. R.T. France, *Reading the Gospels, Matthew*, ed. D. A Carson et al., *New Bible Commentary: 21st Century Edition* (Downers Grove, IL: InterVarsity Press, 2010), page 943.

15. *You say you trust in the Lord, but where is He now?* **Have you ever experienced this type of ridicule, or even had these kinds of thoughts yourself during times of hardship or suffering? How did you respond (to others, or to your own thoughts)?**

APPLY:

1. What did today's reading teach you about God *(any member of the Trinity)* **and His character?**

2. How do the things you've learned today change your heart?

- How do these truths shape or change your view of God?
- Has today's Scripture convicted you of any sin or wrong beliefs that you need to confess?
- Has the Holy Spirit revealed any changes that you need to make in your thoughts, beliefs, or behavior in order to walk in this truth?

Day 3

READ: PSALM 22

Because we are following the order of this psalm, we are going slightly out of order this week according to the events of Jesus' life. So today we are looking back at the things that preceded Christ's crucifixion.

1. Fill in the blanks from verse 11 below:

"Be not _____ from me,
for _____ is near,
and there is _____ to help."
(Psalm 22:11 ESV)

2. What reasons does the psalmist give for asking the Lord to be near?

3. How does the psalmist describe his enemies (vv. 12-13)? Does he have anyone to help him face those enemies (v. 11b)?

READ: MARK 14:26-31

4. In verse 27, what did Jesus tell His disciples would happen? Did it apply to all or only some of them?

5. What was Peter's response (v. 29)?

6. Jesus made sure that Peter knew he wasn't exempt from the original statement by giving him a specific sign to look for. What did He say Peter would do, and what was the sign (v. 30)?

7. How did Peter respond this time? How did all of the other disciples respond?

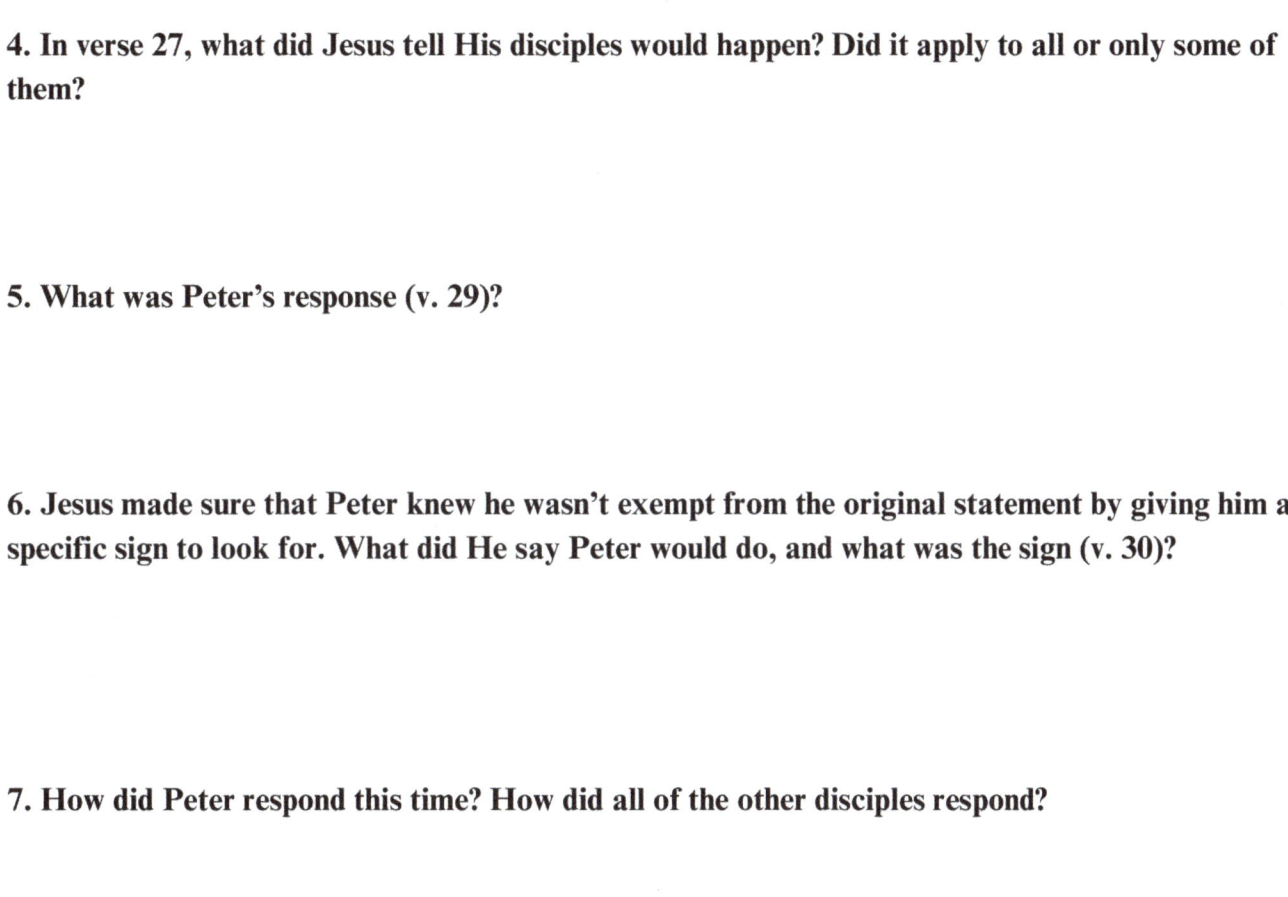

READ: MARK 14:43-50

8. Summarize the events of verses 43-46.

9. What did Peter do in defense of Jesus (v. 47)? *(Though Mark doesn't give the identity of this disciple, John 18:10 tells us it was Peter.)*

10. Keeping your place in Mark, look up Matthew 26:51-56 and answer the following questions:

- What reason(s) did Jesus give for telling Peter to put his sword away?

- What reason did Jesus give for allowing these things to be done to Him (v. 54, 56; see also Mark 14:49)?

- Compare Matthew 26:56 and Mark 14:50. What statement is made in both accounts, and who is it about?

11. Go back to our passage in Mark 14. Who claimed they would never deny the Lord (see v. 31)? Who abandoned Him out of fear (see v. 50)?

We tend to put a lot of emphasis on Peter's arrogance and denial of Christ, but each of the disciples was equally guilty. They *all* shared in Peter's pride as well as in his failure.

THE SPIRIT INDEED
IS WILLING, BUT
THE FLESH IS WEAK.
MARK 14:38

READ: MARK 14:32-42

12. What warning did Jesus give to Peter, James, and John when He returned from praying and found them sleeping? Fill in the blanks from verse 38 below.

"_____ and _____ that you may not enter into
_____. The spirit indeed is _____,
but the flesh is _____."
(Mark 14:38, ESV)

Jesus knew the great temptation His disciples were about to face, and gave them this opportunity to prepare for it.

13. How might things have gone differently for the disciples when they were tempted to desert Jesus had they heeded His instruction to "watch and pray"?

14. What warning can we take from this account concerning arming and protecting ourselves through prayer? Look up the following verses and write any thoughts you have below.

- Ephesians 6:18

- Colossians 4:2

- 1 Peter 5:8

APPLY:

1. What did today's reading teach you about God *(any member of the Trinity)* **and His character?**

2. How do the things you've learned today change your heart?

- How do these truths shape or change your view of God?
- Has today's Scripture convicted you of any sin or wrong beliefs that you need to confess?
- Has the Holy Spirit revealed any changes that you need to make in your thoughts, beliefs, or behavior in order to walk in this truth?

Day 4

READ: PSALM 22

1. Are there any metaphors in verses 14-15 that stand out to you? Note them below, and what you think the author meant by them, and/or what they might point to regarding Christ.

I hope you always feel free to pause and look up unfamiliar words or to do your own research when a verse or passage feels confusing to you. I've chosen just a couple of these things to highlight from Psalm 22:14-15, but if you are unsure of any of the other metaphors or statements, go look those up, too! **If you don't have time right now, be sure to note them somewhere so you can come back to them as time allows.** Slowing down and researching things you don't understand is a huge part of becoming a good student of God's Word!

2. When you say that something melts your heart, what do you usually mean? This expression held a much different meaning when the Bible was written! Look up Deuteronomy 20:8, Joshua 14:8, and Isaiah 13:7, then write a definition of this metaphor in the space below, according to how the biblical authors used it.

Depending on which version of the Bible you're reading from, verse 15 may contain an unfamiliar word. The ESV says, "my strength is dried up like a potsherd." Other versions, like the CSB, say something like, "my strength is dried up like baked clay." The original Hebrew word, ḥereś, means a fragment of earthenware[1]—like a piece broken from a clay pot or dish.

---

1. "H2789 - ḥereś - Strong's Hebrew Lexicon (ESV)." Blue Letter Bible. Accessed 18 May, 2023.
https://www.blueletterbible.org/lexicon/h2789/esv/wlc/0-1/.

3. With this in mind, read the next line of verse 15, and describe below how the writer of this psalm must have been feeling, both physically and emotionally. *(The wording varies a bit again, depending on which translation you're reading, but the basic idea is the same.)*

READ: JOHN 19:14-18

It may be helpful to keep a bookmark in Psalm 22 if you're not already!

4. What mode of execution did the people demand for Jesus?

Verse 18 tells us that Jesus was crucified between two others. Crucifixion is a horrifying and excruciating way to die. The body is so stretched by its own weight as it hangs that all of its bones are pulled out of joint. This should bring to mind a line from the psalm we just read.

5. Fill in the blanks from Psalm 22:14 below:

> *"I am poured out like water,*
> *and ____ my _____ are ____ ___ _____..."*
> *(Psalm 22:14, ESV)*

Take a moment to consider this beautiful thought from Matthew Henry before moving on:

> *"His bones were put out of joint that he might put the whole creation into joint again, which sin had put out of joint, and might make our broken bones to rejoice."*[2]

6. We will look at this more closely next week, but to continue looking specifically at Psalm 22, skip ahead in John 19 to verse 28. What is Jesus' complaint as He hangs on the cross? What part of Psalm 22:14-15 does this align with?

---

2. Matthew Henry, *Matthew Henry's Commentary on the Whole Bible* (Peabody, MA: Hendrickson Publishers, 2008), page 614.

READ: JOHN 19: 31-37

It would sometimes take days for someone to actually die by crucifixion. In order to speed up their death, soldiers were ordered to break the legs of Jesus and those who were crucified with Him. Next week we will dig into why Jesus' legs could not be broken according to Scripture, but I wanted you to read this whole section for the sake of context.

7. What did one of the soldiers do when he saw that Jesus had already died (v. 34)?

8. What happened when he did this, and why is it significant?

John's intention in including this detail is to affirm the physical reality of Jesus' death[3]. Some would say that Jesus only *appeared* to die[4], but here John is emphatic about the fact that Jesus had a real, physical body, which *fully died* on the cross.

9. Turn back to Psalm 22. What line from verses 14-15 matches this event, of blood and water pouring out?

10. Fill in the following blanks from verse 15:

"…you lay me in the _____ of _____."
(Psalm 22:15b, ESV)

We will end our time together with another quote from Matthew Henry's commentary on Psalm 22:

---

3. Donald Guthrie, *Reading the Gospels, John*, ed. D. A Carson et al., *New Bible Commentary: 21st Century Edition* (Downers Grove, IL: InterVarsity Press, 2010), page 1062.
4. Britannica, T. Editors of Encyclopaedia. "Docetism." Encyclopedia Britannica, Accessed 18 May, 2023. https://www.britannica.com/topic/Docetism.

*"The sentence of death passed upon Adam was thus expressed: **Unto dust thou shalt return** [see Genesis 3:19]. And therefore Christ, having an eye to that sentence in his obedience to death, here [in Psalm 22:15] uses a similar expression: **Thou hast brought me to the dust of death.**"*[5]

Truly, Jesus paid it all—all to Him we owe.

APPLY:

1. What did today's reading teach you about God *(any member of the Trinity)* **and His character?**

2. How do the things you've learned today change your heart?

- How do these truths shape or change your view of God?
- Has today's Scripture convicted you of any sin or wrong beliefs that you need to confess?
- Has the Holy Spirit revealed any changes that you need to make in your thoughts, beliefs, or behavior in order to walk in this truth?

---

5. Matthew Henry, *Matthew Henry's Commentary on the Whole Bible* (Peabody, MA: Hendrickson Publishers, 2008), page 614.

Day 5

READ: PSALM 22

1. **Read verses 16-18 closely, writing down each description or metaphor to complete the <u>left</u> side of the following chart. I've filled in the first one to get you started.** *(We will come back to this chart in a moment for the New Testament portion, so don't worry about that side right now.)*

VERSE	PSALMIST'S DESCRIPTION	VERSE	CHRIST'S FULFILLMENT
Ps. 22:16	Dogs encompass me; a company of evildoers encircles me	Mk. 15:16-19	Soldiers surrounding and mocking Him

READ: MARK 15:16-32 & JOHN 19:16-24

There will be some overlap between the two passages, but each gives us slightly different details.

2. Compare the different accounts and do your best to note how each line of Psalm 22:16-18 was fulfilled through Christ's experience during His crucifixion, filling in the remainder of the above chart. *(You should end up with one description seemingly unfulfilled. However, there are more than one that are implied but not explicitly stated in the accounts of Jesus' death, so just do your best and don't stress about it if you're not able to complete the chart!)*

3. Look up Genesis 2:25; 3:7, 10-11. What immediate consequence of sin is described here?

It is not directly stated that Christ was naked when He was crucified (though Scripture does say that the soldiers took His clothes), but that was the typical treatment of those who suffered this humiliating death. We see in Genesis that the shame of nakedness came in with sin. Therefore, He who was made sin for us bore even that shame as He hung on the cross, in order to roll away our reproach and clothe us with His perfect robe of righteousness.

The casting of lots for a criminal's clothing is not something there is evidence for during this time in history[1], so this is a very specific prophecy and an incredible instance of the fulfillment of Old Testament Scripture through Christ.

READ: JOHN 20:24-29

4. Look back at the chart at the beginning of today's study. Did you notice the fulfillment of any remaining spaces as you read this passage in John? Take a moment to finish filling in your chart!

When reading of Jesus' crucifixion, none of the gospel accounts actually state that He was nailed to the cross, but the statement Thomas makes here in John 20:25 implies that the soldiers must have "pierced [His] hands and feet," (Psalm 22:16).

---

1. John H. Walton, Victor H. Matthews, & Mark W. Chavalas, *The IVP Bible Background Commentary: Old Testament* (Downers Grove, IL: InterVarsity Press, 2000), page 524.

READ: PSALM 22:19-31

5. What would you title these remaining two sections of Psalm 22?

- Verses 19-21

- Verses 22-31

6. Read Psalm 22:1-2 again; how was David feeling when he began writing this psalm? What did he do with those feelings?

7. Now continue reading in verses 3-5; how did David respond to his emotions?

David continues the psalm by giving very vivid descriptions of his suffering, but we again see him turn his heart and mind to the Lord as the psalm comes to an end.

8. What did David ask of the Lord in verses 19-21? What do these requests reveal about his heart?

> FOR HE HAS NOT DESPISED OR ABHORRED THE AFFLICTION OF THE AFFLICTED, & HE HAS NOT HIDDEN HIS FACE FROM HIM, BUT HAS HEARD, WHEN HE CRIED TO HIM.
> PSALM 22:24

9. Read through the remainder of the psalm again (verses 22-31) and write down everything the text tells you about God and His character. *Some things will be directly stated and some will only be implied, so take your time to draw out these truths.*

10. Read verses 27-29 again, then look up Philippians 2:5-11 and finish the following statements:

- *Christ did not count equality with God a thing to be _____. (v. 6)*
- *Christ _____ Himself, taking the form of a _____. (v. 7)*
- *Christ _____ Himself by becoming _____ to the point of death. (v. 8)*
- *God has highly _____ Christ and given Him the name that is _____ every name. (v. 9)*
- *At the name of Jesus, _____ knee will bow. (v. 10)*
- *_____ tongue will confess that Jesus Christ is _____, to the glory of God the Father. (v. 11)*

Though the second half of this psalm does not contain any direct prophecies about Christ, this passage in Philippians makes it clear that He is the ultimate answer and fulfillment even of this portion of David's prayer! I want to wrap up our time in Psalm 22 with a quote from one of my favorite commentaries, providing us with some helpful application:

> *"What arose from suffering, and then prophetically explored a unique suffering [Christ's], can now reach down to our often desperate trials. We too can learn to cry out to God (1-8, 11-18), to find comfort and assurance in what is true about us (9) and what we have learned of the truth (10), and to face the future with confidence (22-31) because he will prove himself faithful."*[2] —*J.A. Motyer*

"[WE CAN] FACE THE FUTURE WITH CONFIDENCE BECAUSE [GOD] WILL PROVE HIMSELF FAITHFUL." —J.A. MOTYER

2. J.A. Motyer, *The Psalms*, ed. D. A Carson et al., *New Bible Commentary: 21st Century Edition* (Downers Grove, IL: InterVarsity Press, 2010), page 499.

APPLY:

1. What did today's reading teach you about God *(any member of the Trinity)* **and His character?**

2. How do the things you've learned today change your heart?

- How do these truths shape or change your view of God?
- Has today's Scripture convicted you of any sin or wrong beliefs that you need to confess?
- Has the Holy Spirit revealed any changes that you need to make in your thoughts, beliefs, or behavior in order to walk in this truth?

Week 6

CHRIST'S TRIAL, CRUCIFIXION, & DEATH

SCRIPTURE TO MEMORIZE: PSALM 31:5

Into your hand
I commit my spirit;
You have redeemed me,
O Lord, faithful God

PSALM 31:5

READ: PSALM 69:1-4

Until last week, we had been following Jesus' life as chronologically as possible. Because I wanted to keep all of Psalm 22 together, it may feel like we have backtracked a bit this week as we take a second look at some of the same events and see how they were prophesied in other psalms.

1. Are there any words or phrases that were confusing to you as you read these verses? If so, note them below.

2. Have you ever experienced the feelings the psalmist describes in verses 1-3, specifically in regard to how others were speaking about him (v. 4)? Describe your experience below.

3. What was your response to those who were slandering you? What were your private prayers like during that time? *We will work through this more thoroughly in the coming days, but it may be helpful to begin thinking through it now.*

4. Of the verses that we read today, verse 4 is the part that is especially messianic—pointing to and having been fulfilled in Christ. How does the last line of this verse apply to Christ?

READ: LUKE 23:13-22

We read this on day 2 of last week, so much of it will simply serve to reinforce what we've already been learning. But it is always beneficial to read a text more than once, especially as we strive to keep smaller pieces within their broader context.

5. Jesus was not found guilty of any of the charges brought against Him. What reason(s) might the chief priests, the rulers, and the people have had to hate Him and "attack [Him] with lies," as the psalmist says?

READ: JOHN 15:18-27

This actually took place *before* Jesus was arrested and crucified, but I hope you noticed in verse 25 that He directly quoted Psalm 69:4 as He prepared His disciples for the rejection and persecution they would soon face on His behalf.

6. What/who does John mean by "the world" in this passage?

7. If the world hates you, in what can you find comfort and strength (v. 18)?

8. Why does the world hate and persecute those who follow Jesus (v. 21)?

9. Fill in the following blanks from verses 22 and 24:

"If I had not _____ and _____ to them, they would not have been _____ of _____, but now they have ____ _____ for their _____." (John 15:22, ESV)

"If I had not _____ among them the _____ that ____ _____ _____ did, they would not be _____ of _____, but now they have _____ and _____ both ____ and ____ _____." (John 15:24, ESV)

10. Jesus says that the world hates both Him and His Father (vv. 23-24). Why is it impossible to love one and hate the other?

11. Sometimes people try to pit the two against each other, claiming that the God of the Old Testament is not the same God that Christ reveals Himself to be in the New Testament. Is this accurate, or even possible? Why or why not?

12. Hopefully in question 5 you picked up on the fact that Jesus' enemies didn't really have a good reason to hate Him (other than their sin nature). What ultimate reason does verse 25 give for their hatred?

13. Who does Jesus shift His focus to at the end of this section (v. 26)?

14. What two names does Jesus give the Holy Spirit?

15. What will the Holy Spirit do (v. 26b)?

16. What will Jesus' disciples do, and why are they qualified to do so (v. 27)?

Throughout his Gospel, John uses the term "the world" to refer to unbelievers—"the moral order apart from God. There is a deep chasm between the world's love of its own and its hatred of all that Jesus stood for."[1] The persecution of Jesus by the religious leaders and the rest of the people could be attributed to ignorance of who Jesus really was and Who He represented in His work here on earth, yet He says they are without excuse (John 15:22, 24). They had seen His works and heard His teaching *firsthand*. His coming to earth and living and working among them brought upon the people a moral responsibility as they chose to accept or reject Him.

It is important to note that, like Christ, the Holy Spirit goes out from God the Father (John 15:26). He bears the authority and power of God Himself, being an equal member of the Trinity. The disciples were given the responsibility of being eyewitnesses to all that Jesus had done on earth, and here in John 15, Jesus wanted to reassure them that the Spirit would testify to them as they testified to Jesus. But the promise of the Holy Spirit has a wider application for all Christians throughout the ages. Though we have not seen Jesus face to face as these disciples did, we are still commanded to spread the good news of the gospel by bearing witness to His works in our own lives until He returns.

When we face rejection, persecution, or hatred from the world, it is easy to try to justify ourselves by the fact that we have given no cause for such treatment. But seeing how Christ Himself was treated should encourage us not to seek justification for ourselves, but to patiently endure, trusting our faithful Creator to make all things right, to the glory of His name.

> *"Beloved, do not be surprised at the fiery trial when it comes upon you to test you, as though something strange were happening to you. **But rejoice insofar as you share Christ's sufferings, that you may also rejoice and be glad when his glory is revealed. If you are insulted for the name of Christ, you are blessed, because the Spirit of glory and of God rests upon you.** But let none of you suffer as a murderer or a thief or an evildoer or as a meddler. Yet if anyone suffers as a Christian, let him not be ashamed, but **let him glorify God in that name.** … **Therefore let those who suffer according to God's will entrust their souls to a faithful Creator while doing good.**"*
> *(1 Peter 4:12-16, 19; emphasis mine)*

---

1. Donald Guthrie, *Reading the Gospels, John*, ed. D. A Carson et al., *New Bible Commentary: 21st Century Edition* (Downers Grove, IL: InterVarsity Press, 2010), page 1057.

APPLY:

1. What did today's reading teach you about God *(any member of the Trinity)* **and His character?**

2. How do the things you've learned today change your heart?

- How do these truths shape or change your view of God?
- Has today's Scripture convicted you of any sin or wrong beliefs that you need to confess?
- Has the Holy Spirit revealed any changes that you need to make in your thoughts, beliefs, or behavior in order to walk in this truth?

Day 2

I hope you'll remember that we studied verse 8 during week 2, so today we will only give it a quick glance as we focus on verses 7 and 9.

1. Fill in the blanks with today's verses:

*"For it is for _____ _____ that I have borne _____,
that _____ has covered my face.
For zeal for your house has _____ me,
and the _____ of those who _____ you have fallen on me."*
(Psalm 69:7, 9, ESV)

2. If you initially read today's passage in a different version, you might have missed the repetition; what word appears three times in these short verses?

3. What two things does the psalmist say he is bearing for the sake of God (v. 7)?

FOR CHRIST DID NOT PLEASE HIMSELF, BUT AS IT IS WRITTEN, "THE REPROACHES OF THOSE WHO REPROACHED YOU HAVE FALLEN ON ME."
ROMANS 15:3

4. Though the words *reproach* and *dishonor* are similar, they do have slightly different meanings and connotations (the original Hebrew words are different as well!). Look up both words in a dictionary *(or look back at your chart on page 76)* **and compare/contrast their definitions below.**

- Reproach

- Dishonor

READ: ROMANS 15:1-7

5. What obligation falls upon those who are spiritually strong (v. 1a)?

6. What is this obligation posed in contrast to (v. 1b)?

7. Whose good are we commanded to seek, and to what purpose (v. 2)?

8. What reason are we given for this (v. 3a)?

9. Keeping your place in Romans 15, look up Philippians 2:4-8. How did Christ live out this obligation to bear with the weak and to seek the good of others? To what extent did He go to serve us?

10. Going back to Romans 15, why does verse 4 say the Old Testament was written?

11. How does the Old Testament instruct and encourage us to endure and to bear with the weak? How does it give us hope? *(Verses 5-6 may be helpful in answering this question.)*

12. What command is this section concluded with (v. 7a)?

13. What is the ultimate purpose of this command to foster a spirit of unity in our relationships with one another (v. 6b, 7b)?

Don't miss the significance of this, friend. Christ humbled Himself and came to earth as a human, took the place of a servant, and bore the reproach that you and I deserved. *This* is why we are obligated to bear with the weak as we seek to aid in their spiritual growth. While we were still His enemies, Christ laid down His very life so that we could be welcomed as God's children. *This* is the manner in which we are commanded to welcome one another.

"MAY THE GOD OF ENDURANCE AND ENCOURAGEMENT GRANT YOU TO LIVE IN SUCH HARMONY WITH ONE ANOTHER, IN ACCORD WITH CHRIST JESUS, <u>THAT TOGETHER YOU MAY WITH ONE VOICE GLORIFY THE GOD AND FATHER OF OUR LORD JESUS CHRIST.</u>"
(ROMANS 15:5-6, EMPHASIS ADDED)

14. Whose weaknesses have you been called to bear with for their good and God's glory? What is one practical way you can do this today?

APPLY:

1. What did today's reading teach you about God *(any member of the Trinity)* **and His character?**

2. How do the things you've learned today change your heart?

- How do these truths shape or change your view of God?
- Has today's Scripture convicted you of any sin or wrong beliefs that you need to confess?
- Has the Holy Spirit revealed any changes that you need to make in your thoughts, beliefs, or behavior in order to walk in this truth?

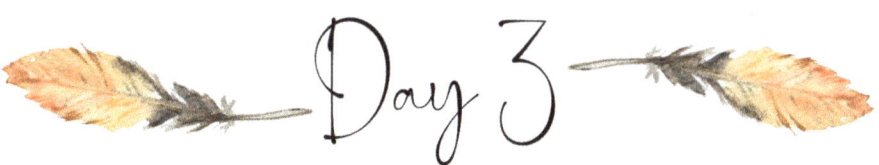

Day 3

READ: PSALM 2:6

If you'll remember, we already spent time on this verse during week 3, so we will only take a brief look at it again today.

1. Who does this verse say the Lord has set on His holy hill?

READ: JOHN 19:19-22

2. What inscription did Pilate have made to hang on Jesus' cross?

3. What group of people does verse 20 specifically name as having read the inscription?

4. What languages was this inscription written in? Why do you suppose Pilate had it written in so many different languages?

5. What did the chief priests ask Pilate to change the sign to say? Why did this distinction matter to them?

6. In what way(s) does this fulfill Psalm 2:6?

READ: PSALM 69:21

7. What does the psalmist say his enemies gave him for food?

8. What was he given to quench his thirst?

READ: MATTHEW 27:34

9. What was Jesus offered as He hung on the cross?

10. Do you know what gall is? Depending on your translation, Psalm 69:21 may have also used this unfamiliar word (the ESV says poison). If you, like me, are not sure of its meaning, look it up in a dictionary and write a definition below:

11. Why do you think Jesus refused to drink the gall He was offered?

Mark 15:23 tells us this particular mixture involved myrrh. Wine mixed with bitter herbs like myrrh was used to dull pain, and was often given to people suffering in order to ease their pain at death. When Jesus refused to drink this mixture, He was effectively refusing to numb the excruciating pain He went through on our behalf.

> *"Sin against a holy God required extreme punishment, and, in order to completely fulfill His position as our substitute, Jesus wanted nothing that took away from that punishment. On the cross, Jesus became sin for us (2 Corinthians 5:21). To accept wine with gall would lessen sin's punishment, and Jesus had come to bear the full brunt of God's wrath against sin, not to take an easier way out (Isaiah 53:10)."[1]*

READ: JOHN 19:28-30

12. What reason does verse 28 give for Jesus saying, "I thirst," at this point in time?

13. Had Psalm 69:21 already been fulfilled when Christ was offered gall but refused to drink it? Why or why not?

14. What does verse 30 say were Christ's final words before He died?

15. What is the significance of this statement?

JESUS HAD COME TO BEAR THE FULL BRUNT OF GOD'S WRATH AGAINST SIN, NOT TO TAKE AN EASIER WAY OUT.

---

1. "What Is Gall in the Bible?" January 4, 2022, https://www.gotquestions.org/gall-in-the-Bible.html.

Many of those standing nearby would have been Jews who knew the Old Testament well. They would have taken notice of Jesus' cry of thirst before He uttered His final words. He had promised His disciples before coming to Jerusalem that "everything that is written about the Son of Man by the prophets will be accomplished," (Luke 18:31). Jesus had cried out not long before with the opening line of Psalm 22—"My God, my God, why have you forsaken me?"—and most of the Jewish people around would have remembered how the psalm continues. They would have recognized the fulfillment of Psalm 22:15, in which the psalmist's mouth is parched and dry.[2]

The sour wine that Jesus drank at the end of His life fulfills the more specific prophecy of Psalm 69:21, and provided His mouth with just enough moisture that He was able to give His final, victorious cry—"It is finished"—before committing His spirit into the hands of the Father (see Luke 23:46).

Throughout His time on earth, Jesus took care to obediently follow the Father's plan, and His suffering and death were no different. There were many incredibly specific prophecies concerning the Messiah, and Jesus perfectly fulfilled each of them. He had just spent hours covered in the filth and shame of our sin, bearing our punishment, becoming sin for us, taking the curse of sin upon Himself, though He Himself knew no sin. Now it was all finished. The price was paid in full, our redemption complete.

APPLY:

1. What did today's reading teach you about God *(any member of the Trinity)* **and His character?**

2. How do the things you've learned today change your heart?

- How do these truths shape or change your view of God?
- Has today's Scripture convicted you of any sin or wrong beliefs that you need to confess?
- Has the Holy Spirit revealed any changes that you need to make in your thoughts, beliefs, or behavior in order to walk in this truth?

---

2. Hope Bolinger, "How Did Jesus Fulfill Prophecy by Saying 'I Thirst'?" March 29, 2021, https://www.christianity.com/wiki/holidays/how-did-jesus-fulfill-prophecy-by-saying-i-thirst.html.

Day 4

READ: PSALM 31:1-5

We're going to begin today with one of my favorite Bible study exercises! One of the biggest reasons we should read and study God's Word is to know *Him* better. Because of this, I find it really beneficial when I'm studying to list out everything a passage reveals to me about His character and nature.

1. List as many things as you can glean from these verses about who God is. Some are directly stated and others are implied. Take your time and be thorough!

VERSE	TRUTH ABOUT GOD

2. How is David's heart guided to a place of total surrender to the Lord as he remembers all of these truths about who God is?

READ: LUKE 23:44-49

Here we are again reading an account of Jesus' final moments before death. There are some variations in detail between the different Gospel accounts, and it is important to remember that the Scriptures never contradict themselves. In this instance, the different authors simply had unique purposes, focuses, and perspectives as they wrote their accounts of Jesus' earthly life.

3. What does Luke record as Jesus' final words (v. 46)?

4. What heart posture does this reveal in Jesus, especially considering the context of the psalm He quoted from?

5. Look up the passages listed below and answer the questions following each:

- **John 6:38-40:**
  - What did Jesus come to earth to do (v. 38)?

  - What two things does Jesus say are the will of God the Father (vv. 39-40)?

- **John 8:28-29**
  - Under whose authority did Jesus work while He lived on earth (v. 28)?

  - What is God's response to obedience (v. 29b)?

- **John 14:31**
  - Whose commands did Jesus say He followed?

  - Why did Jesus obey God the Father during His earthly life?

- **Luke 22:42-43**
  - Did Jesus follow His own will while on earth (v. 42)?

  - What did He receive as a result of His submission (v. 43)?

- **Philippians 2:6-8**
  - What two specific actions did Jesus take in order to obey God the Father (v. 7a, 8a)?

  - How far did Jesus take His obedience (v. 8b)?

Not only as He approached His crucifixion, but *throughout* His earthly life, Jesus demonstrated perfect trust in the Father, fully committed to obeying His will. His words and actions even while hanging on the cross show us that truly He was "obedient to the point of death," (Philippians 2:8). This is massively important, because the will of the Father and the very reason Christ came—to bring eternal life to all who believe on His name—hinged on His perfect obedience to the Father while He lived on earth.

With His final heart cry of, "Father, into your hands I commit my spirit!" Jesus teaches us to use the language of Scripture to give words to our suffering. Even more importantly, this final prayer shows us His continued dependence upon God the Father, even at death. We cannot more effectively care for our souls than to commit them into God's hands for sanctification and grace during our time on earth, and even at our death, trusting that we will finally be made perfect in holiness.[1]

6. How does Jesus' life encourage you to humbly submit your will to the Lord?

7. What area of your life do you need to lay down in obedience today?

APPLY:

1. What did today's reading teach you about God *(any member of the Trinity)* **and His character?**

2. How do the things you've learned today change your heart?

- How do these truths shape or change your view of God?
- Has today's Scripture convicted you of any sin or wrong beliefs that you need to confess?
- Has the Holy Spirit revealed any changes that you need to make in your thoughts, beliefs, or behavior in order to walk in this truth?

---

1. Matthew Henry, *Matthew Henry's Commentary on the Whole Bible* (Peabody, MA: Hendrickson Publishers, 2008), page 1522.

READ: PSALM 34:19-22

1. What does verse 19 say the righteous will face?

2. It can be easy to fall into a sort of "karma" mindset (even subconsciously), where we think if we live the right way, our lives will be free of trouble. Look up John 16:33; what does Jesus tell us we will have in this world?

Even before His death and resurrection, Jesus was looking ahead to the victory He knew He would gain over sin, pain, and death. We can follow this example in our own lives as we live in the tension of what many call "the already but not yet;" Christ has already overcome the world, but He has not yet returned to make all things new. Still we can know with certainty that we *will* be delivered from the trouble of this world one day, because He has already won the war! *"Many are the afflictions of the righteous, but the Lord delivers him out of them all,"* (Psalm 34:19).

3. Back to Psalm 34, what does verse 20 prophesy about Jesus?

4. If God could raise Him from the dead, surely He could have healed broken bones! Why did it matter that none of Christ's bones were broken?
(Don't worry if you're not sure; we'll spend some time digging into this in a bit!)

"IN THE WORLD [THE RIGHTEOUS] MUST HAVE TRIBULATION, THAT THEY MAY BE CONFORMED BOTH TO THE WILL OF GOD AND TO THE EXAMPLE OF CHRIST."
—MATTHEW HENRY

137

READ: JOHN 19:31-36

The brutal procedure of breaking the legs of criminals was not part of the punishment of crucifixion, but rather was used to bring about their deaths more quickly, actually shortening the time of suffering. Without this, death could be delayed for many hours or even days.[1] The Jews wanted to ensure that the bodies of these men would be taken down in time for observance of the Sabbath, so they put in this request to Pilate to have the legs of the three crucified men broken.

5. Why didn't the soldiers break Jesus' legs (v. 33)?

6. What greater reason does verse 36 give for these happenings?

7. Why did John bear witness to these specific details (v. 35b)?

8. Look up 1 Corinthians 5:7. What is Jesus called in this verse?

9. Now look up Exodus 12:43-46. Fill in the blanks below with one of the instructions given concerning the passover lamb:

> *"…you shall not take any of the flesh outside the house,*
> *and you shall not _____ any of its _____."*
> *(Exodus 12:46b, ESV)*

This is just one more way in which the Old Testament was "a shadow of the good things to come," (Hebrews 10:1) and in which Christ perfectly fulfilled every necessary requirement for us to be redeemed from sin. In the same way that the sacrifice of the passover lamb delivered the Israelites from death while they were in Egypt, so Jesus, our perfect Passover Lamb, has delivered us from death by sacrificing Himself on our behalf!

---

1. Donald Guthrie, *Reading the Gospels, John*, ed. D. A Carson et al., *New Bible Commentary: 21st Century Edition* (Downers Grove, IL: InterVarsity Press, 2010), page 1062.

10. Keeping your place in Psalms, look up the following verses and write the blessings or promises given to believers in each:

- Ephesians 1:7

- Romans 8:1

11. Go back to today's psalm (Ps. 34) and look again at verse 22. What does the first half of the verse say the Lord does for His servants?

12. What assurance is given to those who take refuge in the Lord (Ps. 34:22b)?

Through the blood of Jesus we are redeemed, forgiven, and lavished in grace (see Ephesians 1:7-8). When we take refuge in His finished work of salvation, we no longer face condemnation because we have been set free from the law of sin and death (see Romans 8:1-2).

> *"For God has done what the law, weakened by the flesh, could not do. By sending his own Son in the likeness of sinful flesh and for sin, he condemned sin in the flesh, in order that the righteous requirement of the law might be fulfilled in us, who walk not according to the flesh but according to the Spirit."*
> *(Romans 8:3-4)*

THROUGH THE BLOOD OF JESUS WE ARE REDEEMED, FORGIVEN, & LAVISHED IN GRACE. WHEN WE TAKE REFUGE IN HIS FINISHED WORK OF SALVATION, WE NO LONGER FACE CONDEMNATION.

APPLY:

1. What did today's reading teach you about God *(any member of the Trinity)* **and His character?**

2. How do the things you've learned today change your heart?

- How do these truths shape or change your view of God?
- Has today's Scripture convicted you of any sin or wrong beliefs that you need to confess?
- Has the Holy Spirit revealed any changes that you need to make in your thoughts, beliefs, or behavior in order to walk in this truth?

Week 7

CHRIST'S RESURRECTION & ASCENSION

SCRIPTURE TO MEMORIZE: PSALM 16:8

I HAVE SET THE LORD
ALWAYS BEFORE ME
because He is at
my right hand I will
not be Shaken

PSALM 16:8

READ: PSALM 16:8-11

1. In verse 9, the psalmist says he rejoices and dwells in security; what is it that enables him to do so (v. 8)?

2. What two things does the psalmist say he is confident the Lord will not do (v. 10)?

3. Some translations use different words, but most likely, your Bible uses the word *Sheol* in verse 10. Make your best guess as to what this refers to, based on how the psalmist uses it here. *(If you have access to a good Bible dictionary, feel free to look it up!)*

In short, *Sheol* is the term used in the Hebrew Bible to refer to the place of the unrighteous who have died. This word was primarily reserved for usage in poetic contexts and speeches about death, and indicated a serious engagement with the reality of death or mortality. Older versions of the Bible (like the KJV) often translated it as "hell," but it is actually distinct from the hell that is taught of in the New Testament. Newer versions (like the ESV and the CSB) simply leave the word untranslated, as its meaning is much more nuanced than any of the words it could be translated to in our English language. *Sheol* is a place that is set against the work of God, and is the destiny of those who end their lives with no guilt over or repentance of their sin. It can be compared to the place referred to as *Hades* in the New Testament, which is also a place set against God and His kingdom. Revelation tells us that *Hades* will be cast into the lake of fire (see Revelation 20:14). Thus the final destination of those who dwell in either *Sheol* or *Hades*—those who lived in rebellion to God while on earth—is eternal separation from God.[1]

---

1. Chad Brand, *Holman Illustrated Bible Dictionary, Revised and Expanded*, ed. Chad Brand et al. (Nashville, TN: B&H Publishing Group, 2015), pages 1451-1452.

4. How does verse 10 apply to Christ?

READ: MATTHEW 28:1-10 & MARK 16:1-8

If you want to further study and compare the events surrounding Jesus' resurrection, you can find the other two accounts in Luke 24:1-12 and John 20:1-18.

5. Who do Matthew and Mark name as those who went to see Jesus' tomb and anoint His body with spices?

6. What day and time did these things take place?

7. The angel's words to the women are nearly identical in both accounts, though there are a few minor differences. What similar phrase concerning Jesus appears in both Matthew 28:6 and Mark 16:7? *(Hint: it begins with "as.")*

It is significant to see that Jesus had not hidden any of these things from His disciples. He had told them "while he was still in Galilee, that the Son of Man must be delivered into the hands of sinful men and be crucified *and on the third day rise*," (Luke 24:6-7, emphasis added), but John 20:8-9 tells us they did not yet understand.

8. What does the angel tell the women to do (Matt. 28:7; Mark 16:7)?

9. Compare Matthew 28:8 and Mark 16:8. How were the women feeling as they left the tomb?

READ: ACTS 2:22-32

10. Skim through the beginning of this chapter (vv. 1-15). Who is speaking in verses 22-32, and who is he addressing?

11. Whose plan was it for Jesus to be "delivered up" to death (v. 23a)?

12. Who does Peter say crucified Jesus (v. 23b)?

13. Who raised Jesus from the dead (v. 24a)?

14. Would it have been possible for Jesus to have been "held" by death—to have remained dead (v. 24b)?

15. In verse 25, Peter quotes Psalm 16:8-11; who does he say these verses are actually about?

16. Read verse 29 again. Why could Psalm 16 (specifically verse 10) NOT have been referring to David?

17. David knew and believed God's promise to keep one of his descendants on the throne of Israel. With this knowledge what did he foresee and speak about (vv. 30-31)?

18. Who does Peter say are witnesses of Jesus' resurrection (v. 32)?

19. While we who live today are of course not eyewitnesses of the life, death, and resurrection of Christ, we have witnessed His working in our lives! Why does it matter that we bear witness to what He has done for us?

20. Look up Matthew 28:19-20. Why can we witness boldly, without fear?

21. Turn back to Psalm 16 and fill in the following blanks from verses 9-10:

"I have set the Lord _____ _____ ____;
because ____ ____ at my right hand, I shall not be _____.
Therefore my heart is _____, and my whole being _____;
my flesh also dwells _____."
(Psalm 16:9-10, ESV)

22. How do these truths give you courage to obey the command to share the gospel?

23. How does it steady your heart and mind to know that the Lord is "with you always," "at [your] right hand"? What difference does the Lord's presence make in your everyday life?

APPLY:

1. What did today's reading teach you about God *(any member of the Trinity)* **and His character?**

2. How do the things you've learned today change your heart?

- How do these truths shape or change your view of God?
- Has today's Scripture convicted you of any sin or wrong beliefs that you need to confess?
- Has the Holy Spirit revealed any changes that you need to make in your thoughts, beliefs, or behavior in order to walk in this truth?

READ: PSALM 68:18

Note: I really wanted to keep this verse together (context is king, as they say!), but in an effort to follow the order of events in Jesus' earthly life, it needed to be split up. So today we will only be looking at the first half of Psalm 68:18, and we will study the second half on day 4 of this week.

1. What two things does the first half of Psalm 68:18 say Jesus did?

2. The fulfillment of the first piece is pretty obvious, as we will see when we look at the New Testament accounts of Jesus ascending into heaven. But what does the second part—"leading a host of captives in your train"—mean, and how does it apply to Christ? *Do your best to answer before reading on!*

Paul quotes this verse in Ephesians 4 (which we will study together in a couple of days, but feel free to read it on your own now!), explaining that Jesus first *descended* at His death and burial (see Ephesians 4:9) and then *ascended* "far above all the heavens," (Ephesians 4:10). In His ascension from the grave and, later, into heaven, Jesus demonstrated His authority and power, freeing us—"a host of captives"—from the bondage of sin and death!

READ: LUKE 24:50-53

3. What did Jesus do before leaving the disciples (v. 50)?

4. What happened while He was blessing them (v. 51)?

READ: ACTS 1:6-11

5. What do the disciples ask Jesus in verse 6?

6. Fill in the blanks below with Jesus' answer to their question (v. 7):

> *"He said to them, "It is _____ for _____ to _____ times or seasons that _____ _____ has _____ by his own authority." (Acts 1:7, ESV)*

7. What two things does Jesus tell them instead (v. 8)?

- *You will* _____

  _____

- *You will* _____

  _____

Jesus wanted the disciples to know that while His return was something to eagerly look forward to, it was not what they needed to be worried about. He had other work for them to concern themselves with in His absence, and *that* was to be their priority.

8. What happened next (v. 9)?

9. Who appeared as the disciples "were gazing into heaven" (v. 10)?

> "DISCIPLESHIP IS NOT ABOUT KNOWING THE TIMES AND DATES, BUT IT IS ABOUT BEING READY."[1]
> —CONRAD GEMPF

---

1. Conrad Gempf, *Acts*, ed. D. A Carson et al., *New Bible Commentary: 21st Century Edition* (Downers Grove, IL: InterVarsity Press, 2010), page 1070.

10. What did the men (presumably angels) tell the disciples about Jesus' return (v. 11)?

READ: PSALM 109:8

Keep Acts 1 ready—we'll be coming right back to it!

I know this feels a little out of place after what we just read, but this seemingly random verse will make sense in a moment as we continue reading the narrative of the events that followed Jesus' resurrection!

11. Thinking back to what we previously learned about this verse *(flip back to week 4, day 4 if you aren't sure!)*, **what do you think the second half of this verse is referring to?**

READ: ACTS 1:12-26

12. How many disciples were gathered together, and what were they doing during this time (vv. 14-15)?

13. What reason does Peter give for Judas having betrayed Jesus (v. 16)?

14. In verse 20, Peter quotes two psalms in reference to Judas—Psalm 69:25 and Psalm 109:8. In response to these Scriptures, what does he say the disciples need to do (vv. 21-22)?

15. How do verses 23-26 tell us they selected the one who would take the position Judas had left empty? Who ultimately chose the one who would be added to the twelve apostles?

16. Casting lots is not a method we typically use when making decisions today. In what other way(s) can we imitate the wisdom of these apostles when we need the Lord's direction and guidance?

1. What did today's reading teach you about God *(any member of the Trinity)* **and His character?**

2. How do the things you've learned today change your heart?

- How do these truths shape or change your view of God?
- Has today's Scripture convicted you of any sin or wrong beliefs that you need to confess?
- Has the Holy Spirit revealed any changes that you need to make in your thoughts, beliefs, or behavior in order to walk in this truth?

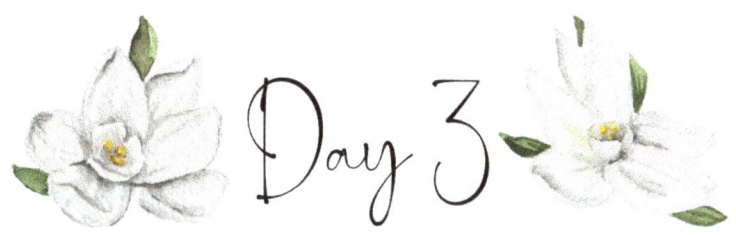

Day 3

READ: PSALM 110:1

1. Fill in the blanks below to name the different people in this verse:
(*Hint: I've color-coded them for you to help you out a bit!*)

_____

_____

_____

_____

"THE LORD SAYS TO MY LORD:
'SIT AT MY RIGHT HAND,
UNTIL I MAKE YOUR ENEMIES
YOUR FOOTSTOOL.'"
(PSALM 110:1, ESV)

_____

_____

2. Where is Jesus invited to sit? For how long?

3. Look up Mark 16:19. What does this verse say Jesus did when He ascended into heaven?
(*It should be noted here that some of the earliest manuscripts of Mark's Gospel stop at verse 8.*)

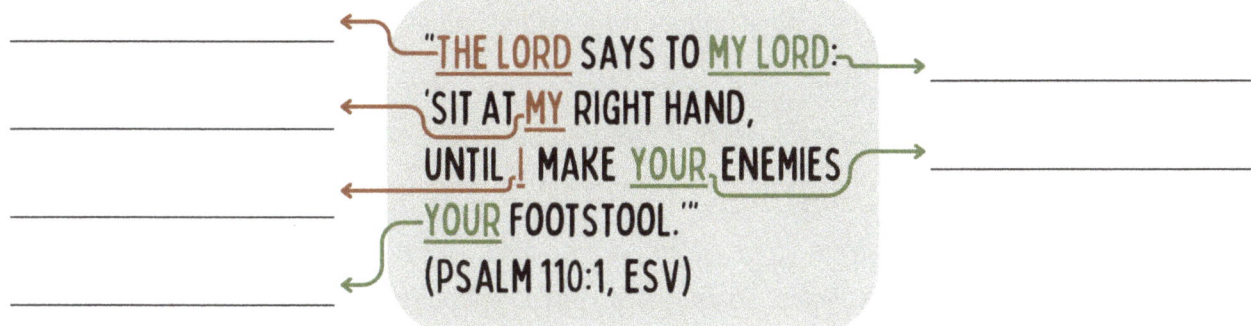

READ: ACTS 2:32-36

4. Give verses 1-13 a quick read-through. What event has given Peter this opportunity to preach to this crowd of Jews?

Peter clarifies to the crowd that "these people are not drunk, as you suppose," (v. 15) but that they are witnesses to the fact that God had raised Jesus to life! He uses this as an opportunity to share the gospel with these Jews gathered in Jerusalem, showing them through the Old Testament Scriptures that there could be no doubt—Jesus was the Messiah that David had predicted.

5. What does Peter say about Jesus in verses 32-33?

- *God _____ Him _____ (v. 32).*
- *He is _____ at the _____ _____ of God (v. 33).*
- *He has _____ the promised _____ _____ (v. 33).*
- *He _____ _____ the things the crowd was seeing and hearing (v. 33).*

6. What was Peter referring to, that Christ had "poured out," and that the crowd was seeing and hearing?

Prior to this, Peter quoted from Psalm 16 as proof that David could not have been the Messiah (which we studied on day 1 of this week, if you'll remember). Here he quotes a different psalm as another piece of evidence that it was impossible for David to have been the Promised One.

7. Using Psalm 110:1, what argument does Peter give about David to further prove his point (vv. 34-35)?

8. Though the Jews viewed Jesus as a criminal, what does Peter say we can know for certain (v. 36)?

READ: HEBREWS 1:1-4, 13

9. What does the writer of Hebrews tell us about Jesus in verse 3?

- *He is the _____ of the _____ of _____.*
- *He is the exact _____ of [God's] _____.*
- *He _____ the universe by the _____ of His _____.*

- *He made _____ for sins.*
- *He is seated at the _____ _____ of the _____ on high.*

10. Why does it matter for us today that Christ is seated at God's right hand? Look up Hebrews 10:11-14 to help with your answer.

1. What did today's reading teach you about God *(any member of the Trinity)* **and His character?**

2. How do the things you've learned today change your heart?

- How do these truths shape or change your view of God?
- Has today's Scripture convicted you of any sin or wrong beliefs that you need to confess?
- Has the Holy Spirit revealed any changes that you need to make in your thoughts, beliefs, or behavior in order to walk in this truth?

Day 4

READ: PSALM 68:18

If you'll remember, we studied the first half of this verse on day 2 of this week; today we will dig into the second half. (So if you happened to skip that day's work or leave it unfinished, I suggest going back to complete it before proceeding!)

1. Fill in the blanks from today's verse below:

> *"You ascended on high,*
> *_____ a host of _____ in your train*
> *and _____ _____ among men,*
> *even among the rebellious, that the Lord God may dwell there."*
> *(Psalm 68:18, ESV)*

2. What do you think the psalmist is referring to (specifically referencing the Messiah) with the two phrases you just filled in? *We will look more closely at this when we turn to today's New Testament passage, but for now, just give it your best guess. <u>Remember it is good and helpful for our growth in understanding to "wrestle" with a text that feels confusing rather than immediately going to others for answers!</u>*

3. Who does the last phrase of this verse say God will dwell among?

156

4. Look up the following verses and answer the questions connected to each:

- **Romans 3:10-12**
  - Who is righteous (v. 10)?

  - Who has turned from God (v. 12)?

- **Romans 3:23**
  - Who has sinned?

- **Ephesians 2:1-3**
  - Who followed the world, walking in trespasses and sins (vv. 1-2)?

  - Who lived in the passions of their flesh (v. 3)?

- **Ephesians 2:4-6**
  - What is God rich in (v. 4)?

  - What did He do for us "because of the great love with which he loved us" (vv. 4-5)?

- **John 14:23**
  - What does Jesus say He and the Father will do for those who love and obey Him?

- **Revelation 21:3**
  - Where has God chosen to make His dwelling place?

There is much more on this topic throughout the Scriptures, but I hope this was enough to help you see what an incredible statement David was making in Psalm 68! We are all rebellious by nature, yet even while we lived as His *enemies* (see Romans 5:8), God loved us enough to send His Son to pay our insurmountable debt so that He could dwell among us. This is truly amazing grace, and should cause us to fall on our faces before Him, overcome with awe and humble gratitude.

READ: EPHESIANS 4:1-16

5. How are believers urged to walk (v. 1)?

6. What does that look like (vv. 2-3)?

7. What has each of us been given (v. 7a)?

8. What is "the measure of Christ's gift" (v. 7b)? Look up Romans 12:3 and Ephesians 4:16 if you need some help.

9. What is the word "therefore" (v. 8) referring to?

10. What does it mean that Christ "led a host of captives" (v. 8)?

THIS IS TRULY AMAZING GRACE, & SHOULD CAUSE US TO FALL ON OUR FACES BEFORE HIM.

11. Based on your answers to the above questions, what does Paul say Psalm 68:18 means? How does he apply this psalm to believers?

You may have noticed that Paul actually changed the wording of the phrase about gifts when he quoted this psalm. There are various reasons scholars believe he may have done this, but the most likely is that his focus was not primarily on the historical reference of the psalm itself, but on its typological fulfillment in Christ![1] Jesus has taken captive the powers that bound us—sin and death, and the rulers of this world—and now bestows the victor's gifts on those He has redeemed (rather than *receiving* those gifts). This is so like our generous God, to grace us with the gifts He has rightly won.

12. What is the purpose of the gifts we receive in Christ (vv. 12-16)?

13. Are you using your gifts for these purposes? If not, what is one change you can make to begin stewarding your gifts well?

APPLY:

1. What did today's reading teach you about God *(any member of the Trinity)* **and His character?**

---

1. Max Turner, *Ephesians*, ed. D. A Carson et al., *New Bible Commentary: 21st Century Edition* (Downers Grove, IL: InterVarsity Press, 2010), page 1238.

2. How do the things you've learned today change your heart?

- How do these truths shape or change your view of God?
- Has today's Scripture convicted you of any sin or wrong beliefs that you need to confess?
- Has the Holy Spirit revealed any changes that you need to make in your thoughts, beliefs, or behavior in order to walk in this truth?

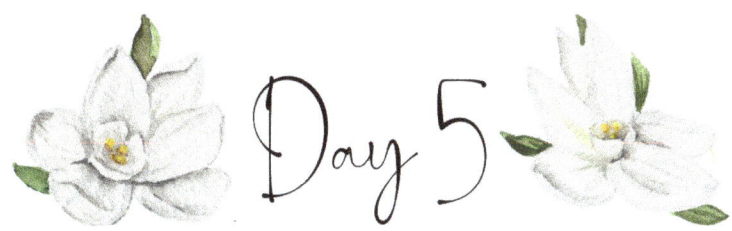

Day 5

READ: PSALM 110

We have already looked at Psalm 110 at a couple of different points during our study (day 4 of week 3, and day 3 of week 7 if you want to look back), so we will not be studying the entire psalm today. But to gain proper context of a verse, it is always a good practice to read the surrounding passage!

This psalm focuses heavily on the Lordship and Kingship of Christ, but there is another role spoken of as well, which can be easy to skip over if you're not paying attention.

1. About what does verse 4 tell us that "the Lord has sworn, and will not change his mind"?

2. One of God's attributes is *immutability*: the inability to change. Considering this, would the Lord be *able* to change His mind—to go back on His word? Explain your answer.

3. Who does verse 4 specifically mention?

4. Keeping your place in Psalm 110, turn to Genesis 14:17-24. Use the space below to note anything you learn about Melchizedek.

5. Why does Psalm 110:4 say Melchizedek's priesthood was "forever"? Was it actually? Why or why not?

6. In what ways does Melchizedek's priesthood give a picture of Christ?
(Do your best to answer before moving on, but if you're not sure, don't worry! We're going to spend the rest of today's study digging into Christ's priesthood together.)

READ: HEBREWS 6:13-20

7. When God made a promise to Abraham, who did He swear by (v. 13)?

8. What two unchangeable things give us assurance of our hope (vv. 17-18)?

"THE PRIESTHOOD OF CHRIST IS CONFIRMED BY THE HIGHEST RATIFICATIONS POSSIBLE, THAT IT MIGHT BE AN UNSHAKEN FOUNDATION FOR OUR FAITH AND HOPE TO BUILD UPON."[1] —MATTHEW HENRY

9. Who does the writer of Hebrews introduce in the final verse of chapter 6?

---

1. Matthew Henry, *Matthew Henry's Commentary on the Whole Bible* (Peabody, MA: Hendrickson Publishers, 2008), page 718.

10. What two names are used to describe Melchizedek in verse 2?

11. In verse 3, is the writer speaking literally or metaphorically about Melchizedek? Explain your answer.

12. According to the Mosaic Law, priests were required to be descended from the tribe of Levi. From what tribe was Jesus descended (vv. 13-14)?

13. How could Jesus become our High Priest if He wasn't a Levite? *(Verses 16-17 may help with your answer.)*

14. Verse 12 tells us that a change in the priesthood necessitates a change in the law. What change in the law did Christ introduce when He became our High Priest?

15. Why did we need a change in the law (vv. 18-19a)?

16. How is the hope we have under the New Covenant better than the former law (v. 19b)?

17. What does verse 22 call Jesus?

18. What prevented the former priests from continuing in office (v. 23)?

THE HOPE WE HAVE IN CHRIST IS <u>BETTER</u> BECAUSE IT ENABLES US TO TRULY DRAW NEAR TO GOD!

19. How long does Christ hold His office of High Priest (v. 24)? Why is this?

20. Fill in the blanks of verse 25:

"_____, he is able to save to the _____ those who
_____ _____ to God _____ him, since he _____ lives to
make _____ for them." (Hebrews 7:25, ESV)

Read that verse again, and really let the words you wrote in the blanks sink in. *Because* "he holds his priesthood permanently," (v. 24), Christ is "able to save to the uttermost"—completely and perfectly. There is no end to the people He can save or the things He can save them from! He "always lives to make intercession" for those who draw near to God through Him. To intercede is *to stand between*. Jesus continually stands between us and God *so that* we can draw near to Him with confidence and receive mercy and grace every time we need it (see Hebrews 4:14-16).

21. Read through verses 26-28 again, and make two lists below, contrasting human priests with the priesthood of Christ.
Note that some characteristics are implied rather than directly stated, and you probably won't fill every blank (but kudos to you if you are able to!). I've done the first one on each side for you to help get you started.

CHRIST

- *holy* _____
- _____
- _____
- _____
- _____
- _____
- _____
- _____
- _____

HUMAN PRIESTS

- *sinful* _____
- _____
- _____
- _____
- _____
- _____
- _____
- _____
- _____

Depending on which translation of the Bible you're reading, verse 28 likely says that Christ has been "perfected" or "made perfect." This wording feels confusing to us after having just read that He is holy (and, therefore, already perfect)! The Greek word used for this phrase is *teleioō*, and it carries the meaning of being complete, accomplished, or fulfilled.[2] One commentary explains it this way:

> *"[Jesus] was **qualified to fulfil** this role or 'made perfect for ever' by means of his obedient life, his sacrificial death and his entrance into the heavenly presence of God."*[3]
> —David Peterson

22. Considering all that we have learned today about Jesus as our perfect and permanent High Priest, turn to Hebrews 4 and write verses 14-16 in the space below:

23. How does it strengthen you in your own struggle against sin to know that you have a perfect High Priest who was tempted just like you and sympathizes with your weaknesses, yet never sinned?

JESUS CONTINUALLY STANDS BETWEEN US & GOD SO THAT WE CAN DRAW NEAR TO HIM WITH CONFIDENCE & RECEIVE MERCY & GRACE EVERY TIME WE NEED IT.

2. G5048 - *teleioō* - Strong's Greek Lexicon (esv)." Blue Letter Bible. Accessed 12 Jul, 2023.
https://www.blueletterbible.org/lexicon/g5048/esv/mgnt/0-1/
3. David Peterson, *Hebrews*, ed. D. A Carson et al., *New Bible Commentary: 21st Century Edition* (Downers Grove, IL: InterVarsity Press, 2010), page 1338, emphasis added.

APPLY:

1. What did today's reading teach you about God *(any member of the Trinity)* **and His character?**

2. How do the things you've learned today change your heart?

- How do these truths shape or change your view of God?
- Has today's Scripture convicted you of any sin or wrong beliefs that you need to confess?
- Has the Holy Spirit revealed any changes that you need to make in your thoughts, beliefs, or behavior in order to walk in this truth?

Week 8

CHRIST'S EXALTATION & GLORIFICATION

SCRIPTURE TO MEMORIZE: PSALM 45:6

Your throne O God
is forever & ever
the Scepter of
Your kingdom
IS A
Scepter of
Uprightness

PSALM 45:6

Day 1

READ: PSALM 45

We will mainly be focusing on verses 6-7 and won't spend a lot of time looking at this entire psalm. But I found myself confused when trying to recognize which portions are messianic, and I thought you might've struggled, too. So I wanted to share this short summary that I found particularly helpful:

> *"This psalm, like all royal psalms, runs beyond what any earthly king could be, to the longed-for Messiah in whom all the glories are true. Likewise it speaks tellingly to the Bride of Christ of her true position, beauty, and dedication."[1] —J.A. Motyer*

1. What characterizes the king's speech (v. 2)?

2. Look up Luke 4:22 and note what it says about Jesus' words. How does this fulfill what is said of the king in Psalm 45:2?

3. Back in Psalm 45; what does verse 6 say about God's throne?

4. Continuing to keep your place in Psalm 45, turn to Luke 1:32-33. Fill in the blanks from the angel's description of Jesus in verse 33:

> *"...he will _____ over the house of Jacob _____,*
> *and of his _____ there will be ____ _____."*
> *(Luke 1:33, ESV)*

---

1. J.A. Motyer, *The Psalms*, ed. D. A Carson et al., *New Bible Commentary: 21st Century Edition* (Downers Grove, IL: InterVarsity Press, 2010), page 515.

5. How does this align with what is said of God in Psalm 45:6?

6. If you haven't already, turn back to Psalm 45. What else does verse 6 tell us about this king? How is his scepter described?

7. How does the king feel about righteousness and wickedness (v. 7)?

8. What do these two aspects together reveal to us about this king and his kingdom?

Uprightness is the guiding principle of this king, the underlying foundation of his kingdom and all that comes of it. This is a kingdom in which not only does righteousness guide and rule, but wickedness *is not tolerated*. Both officially and in his personal life, this king is *holy*.

9. Look up Isaiah 11:1-5. The righteous Branch being referred to is the Messiah—Jesus Christ. Use the space below to list the things by which He and His kingdom are characterized.

THERE SHALL COME FORTH A SHOOT FROM THE STUMP OF JESSE, & A BRANCH FROM HIS ROOTS SHALL BEAR FRUIT.
ISAIAH 11:1

READ: HEBREWS 1:7-9

10. Who is being spoken of in verses 8-9?

11. So then, whose "throne is forever and ever," (v. 8)? Who has been anointed as King (v. 9)?

In Psalm 45, the writer seems to quickly switch back and forth between the people he is addressing, inserting this statement to God in the middle of an address to the king. Yet here in Hebrews, the writer makes it clear that ultimately this psalm—even the statement addressed to God—is about Jesus. This idea of a Messiah who is God and yet also worships God (e.g., "God, *your* God, has anointed you," Psalm 45:7) is a paradox that could only find its resolution in the person of Jesus Christ. The prophesied King and the God of the universe are one and the same, and it is *His* throne that is everlasting.

12. What difference does it make for us as believers that our King will reign forever? Put differently, how would it change things if His reign was only temporary?

APPLY:

1. What did today's reading teach you about God *(any member of the Trinity)* **and His character?**

2. How do the things you've learned today change your heart?

- How do these truths shape or change your view of God?
- Has today's Scripture convicted you of any sin or wrong beliefs that you need to confess?
- Has the Holy Spirit revealed any changes that you need to make in your thoughts, beliefs, or behavior in order to walk in this truth?

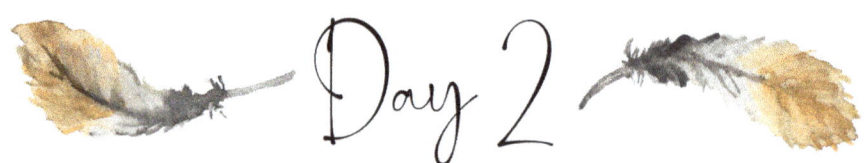

Day 2

READ: PSALM 2

We are coming full-circle during our final week as we go back over two of the same psalms that we studied during week 1! Last time we looked at this passage, we specifically focused on Jesus as the Son of God, as spoken of in Psalm 2:7 (if you want a refresher, flip back to day 3 of week 1). Today and tomorrow we will look at the verses immediately following to see what else this psalm has to teach us about Christ.

1. The Lord is speaking to His Anointed King—His Son (v. 7). What promise does the Father give to the Son in verse 8?

2. Contrast the kings described in verses 1-5 with the King spoken of throughout the remainder of this psalm. What are their attitudes like? What characterizes their behavior?

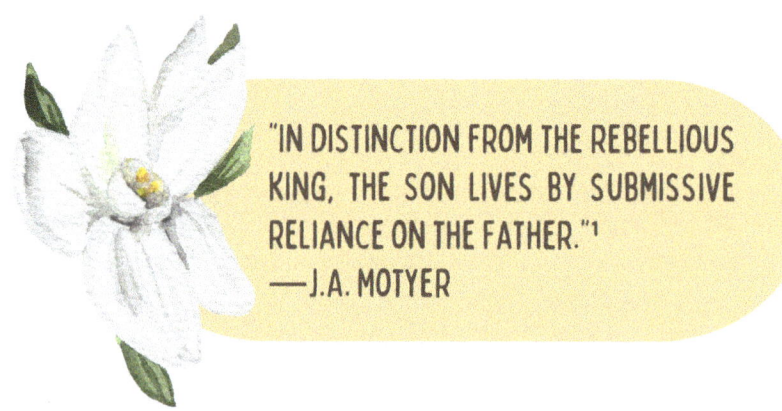

"IN DISTINCTION FROM THE REBELLIOUS KING, THE SON LIVES BY SUBMISSIVE RELIANCE ON THE FATHER."[1]
—J.A. MOTYER

---

1. J.A. Motyer, *The Psalms*, ed. D. A Carson et al., *New Bible Commentary: 21st Century Edition* (Downers Grove, IL: InterVarsity Press, 2010), page 515.

3. What does the outworking of Christ's authority over the earth look like (v. 9)?

4. Who is being broken and dashed to pieces? *Verses 10-12 may be helpful in answering this question.*

READ: JOHN 17:1-5

5. What does Jesus ask the Father for at the end of verse 1?

6. If you are comfortable writing in your Bible, read through verses 1-5 again and mark each occurrence of any form of the word glory. How many times did you find it? *(If there were such a thing as extra credit in this study, you could get it by tracking this repetition throughout the entire chapter rather than just the first five verses!)*

As you can see, this prayer carries the weighty theme of *glory*. Christ prayed this just before His trial, crucifixion, and resurrection, which, as Donald Guthrie said, "is the *pathway* to glory."[2]

7. What does Christ say the Father has given Him (v. 2a)?

8. What does Jesus say is the purpose of the authority He has received (v. 2b)?

9. What is eternal life, according to verse 3?

---

2. Donald Guthrie, *Reading the Gospels, John*, ed. D. A Carson et al., *New Bible Commentary: 21st Century Edition* (Downers Grove, IL: InterVarsity Press, 2010), page 1059, emphasis added.

READ: REVELATION 2:26-27

10. How is Christ seen using His authority in these verses?

11. Fill in the following blanks about those who will receive authority from Christ:

"The one who _____ and who _____ my works _____ the _____, to him I will give authority over the nations…"
(Revelation 2:26, ESV)

12. How do we live as those who conquer and who keep His works? What, practically, does this look like?

13. Verse 25 says to "hold fast what you have." This is one way in which we live victoriously as Christians—but *how* do we hold fast? How can we cling to Christ during our time here on earth?

14. What will it look like when those conquerors are ruling over the nations (v. 27)?

This should sound very familiar to you. It very closely echoes what is said in Psalm 2:9 of what things will be like when the Father gives this authority to the Son! So when we persevere in obedience to Christ, He then actually promises to *share* His authority with us, giving us dominion over the nations. Matthew Henry says this abundant reward of power and dominion over the rest of the world is given to "the persevering victorious believer," and that we must also, therefore, be given the necessary wisdom for *using* such power and dominion.[3] What an incredible promise!

1. What did today's reading teach you about God *(any member of the Trinity)* **and His character?**

2. How do the things you've learned today change your heart?

- How do these truths shape or change your view of God?
- Has today's Scripture convicted you of any sin or wrong beliefs that you need to confess?
- Has the Holy Spirit revealed any changes that you need to make in your thoughts, beliefs, or behavior in order to walk in this truth?

---

3. Matthew Henry, *Matthew Henry's Commentary on the Whole Bible* (Peabody, MA: Hendrickson Publishers, 2008), page 1985.

READ: PSALM 2

1. To pick up where we left off in this psalm yesterday, what is the "therefore" in verse 10 referring to? By what are the kings of the earth to be warned (v. 9)?

2. What is given as the wise response to this warning (v. 11-12)?

> WHEN WE ARE WALKING IN WISDOM & THE FEAR OF THE LORD, WE WILL FIND A PLACE OF REFUGE & SAFETY.

3. What does it mean to "kiss the Son" (v. 12a), and how does it relate to the admonition to serve the Lord given in verse 11?

"There can be no service to the Lord without submission to the Son!"[1] —J.A. Motyer

4. Fill in the following blanks from the end of verse 12:

"_____ are all who _____ _____ in him."
(Psalm 2:12b, ESV)

Based on the warning given in verses 10-12, I think we can infer that those facing destruction in verse 9 are those who are not serving the Lord. Yet if we look at it from the opposite perspective, we can see that when we are walking in wisdom and the fear of the Lord, we will find a place of refuge and safety.

---

1. J.A. Motyer, *The Psalms*, ed. D. A Carson et al., *New Bible Commentary: 21st Century Edition* (Downers Grove, IL: InterVarsity Press, 2010), page 490.

READ: JOHN 3:35-36

5. What two things does verse 35 tell us about the Father and the Son?

6. What does it mean for the Father to have given all things into the Son's hand? Look up John 5:27; 17:1-2 if you need help with your answer.

"The hallmark of Jesus' mission was that the Father loves him and has complete trust in him."[2]
—*Donald Guthrie*

7. What two groups of people are contrasted in verse 36?

- *Whoever _____ in the Son*
- *Whoever does not _____ the Son*

8. What difference does it make to our understanding for belief to be contrasted with *disobedience* rather than unbelief?

I love this choice of wording, because it gets right to the heart of the issue. If we truly believe in Jesus, we *will* be living lives of obedience. If it is someone's practice to walk in disobedience to Christ, we can pretty safely assume that they do not truly *believe* Him. Behavior always follows belief. Regardless of what we know or say, the way we live our daily lives will always betray what we truly *believe*.

BEHAVIOR ALWAYS FOLLOWS BELIEF.

---

2. Donald Guthrie, *Reading the Gospels, John*, ed. D. A Carson et al., *New Bible Commentary: 21st Century Edition* (Downers Grove, IL: InterVarsity Press, 2010), page 1033.

9. Compare Psalm 2:12 with John 3:36. What similarities do you notice? How does Christ fulfill this psalm, specifically toward those who reject Him?

*"God's wrath is not to be regarded as impersonal but as an active principle of God's holiness. The **only** means of avoiding that wrath is by the path of faith."[3] —Donald Guthrie*

READ: REVELATION 19:11-16

10. Use the following charts to list everything these verses tell us about Christ:

VERSE	CHRIST'S APPEARANCE

---

3. Donald Guthrie, *Reading the Gospels, John*, ed. D. A Carson et al., *New Bible Commentary: 21st Century Edition* (Downers Grove, IL: InterVarsity Press, 2010), page 1033, emphasis added.

VERSE	CHRIST'S NAME OR CHARACTER

VERSE	CHRIST'S ACTIONS

11. What causes God's wrath to be poured out? Why is this a good thing?

"THOSE WHO KISS THE SON REMAIN EVER AWARE OF THE FEAR RIGHTLY DUE TO HIM AND THE WRATH THAT IS INSEPARABLE FROM HIS HOLINESS. ... THERE IS NO REFUGE <u>FROM</u> HIM: ONLY <u>IN</u> HIM."[4]
—J.A. MOTYER

12. Do believers need to fear God's judgment? Why or why not?

13. In what way(s) can we take comfort in God's wrath?

---

4. J.A. Motyer, *The Psalms*, ed. D. A Carson et al., *New Bible Commentary: 21st Century Edition* (Downers Grove, IL: InterVarsity Press, 2010), page 490, emphasis added.

APPLY:

1. What did today's reading teach you about God *(any member of the Trinity)* **and His character?**

2. How do the things you've learned today change your heart?

- How do these truths shape or change your view of God?
- Has today's Scripture convicted you of any sin or wrong beliefs that you need to confess?
- Has the Holy Spirit revealed any changes that you need to make in your thoughts, beliefs, or behavior in order to walk in this truth?

Day 4

READ: PSALM 8

1. In which two verses do you find an identical sentence? Write that sentence in the space below:

Repetition like this is one of the easiest ways to recognize themes in the Bible, particularly in poetry like the Psalms. David "bookends" this psalm with these words to direct our focus to the majesty of the Lord, with all of the thoughts in between flowing out of his awe of the Lord's incomparable greatness!

2. Fill in the following blanks from verses 3-4:

"When I look at your _____, the _____ of _____ fingers,
the moon and the stars, which _____ have _____ in place,
what is _____ that _____ are _____ of him,
and the _____ of _____ that _____ _____ for him?"
(Psalm 8:3-4, ESV)

3. What thoughts come to mind as you consider the significance of God's care for us as humans? How does this impact your view of the gospel?

When we read this psalm with the gospel in mind, verses 3-4 really shift our perspective and give us insight into how absolutely unthinkable it is that the very Creator of the world would come to redeem mankind. It is incredible that God in His greatness and majesty would even think of us, and more so that He would also *care* for us. That the Son of God would actually come to be one of us in order to make a way for us to dwell with Him is beyond imagining! Truly, "what is man"? *Yet, God cares for us*—enough to empty Himself and live in the weakness of human flesh, humbly enduring the shame of the cross, and ultimately giving His very life to pay the price of our sin. How majestic is His name in all the earth!

THAT THE SON OF GOD WOULD ACTUALLY COME TO BE ONE OF US IN ORDER TO MAKE A WAY FOR US TO DWELL WITH HIM IS BEYOND IMAGINING! TRULY, "WHAT IS MAN"?
YET, GOD CARES FOR US.

Moving on to verses 5-6; in their immediate context, these verses are speaking of the great privileges the Lord has given to mankind. Yet they are quoted multiple times in the New Testament in reference to Christ.

4. How could verse 5 be true of Christ? Is He "lower than the heavenly beings"?

READ: HEBREWS 2:5-10

5. Upon first reading this passage, what insight does it give you in regard to the previous question? Did you notice the small addition made by the writer of Hebrews (v. 7)?

6. The writer of Hebrews spends the entirety of the first chapter explaining how Jesus is superior to angels. Now here in chapter 2 he says that "for a little while," Jesus was made lower than them (Hebrews 2:7, 9). What is he referring to?

7. We are told here that everything has been put "in subjection under [Christ's] feet" (v. 8a). Yet do we currently see everything in subjection to Him (v. 8b)? How can both things be true?

This is just one aspect in which we dwell in "the already but not yet." Jesus Christ is God, and therefore He is sovereign over all creation, but in our broken and sinful world, "we do not yet see everything in subjection to him," (Hebrews 2:8). As believers, we get to experience the benefits of the coming age in advance as we wait for Christ to return and bring us into the *full* enjoyment of our salvation.

8. With what is Christ crowned "because of the suffering of death" (v. 9)?

9. Why was Jesus made lower than the angels (v. 9)?

10. How does the author of Hebrews refer to Christ in verse 10?

To put these two ideas together, we can see that while death was the pathway to *glory* for Christ, by God's grace it is also the means of *salvation* for us.[1]

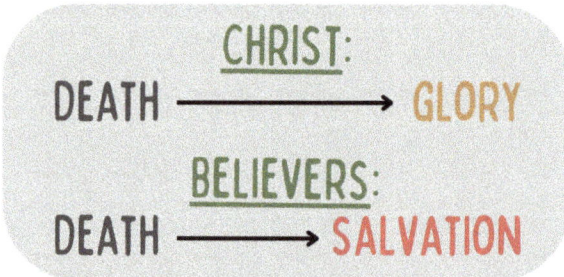

---

1. David Peterson, *Hebrews*, ed. D. A Carson et al., *New Bible Commentary: 21st Century Edition* (Downers Grove, IL: InterVarsity Press, 2010), page 1327.

READ: 1 CORINTHIANS 15:20-28

11. What does verse 25 say Christ must do?

12. What is the last enemy to be destroyed (v. 26)?

13. Verse 27 quotes our psalm about all things being in subjection to Christ, yet the previous verses (as well as our experiences on this earth) make it clear that He has not yet destroyed all of His enemies. How can this be? How does this fit into the "already but not yet" concept mentioned earlier?

In this passage, Paul traces the loss and regaining of paradise, as well as the recovery of the submission of all things to God as in the beginning of Creation. Christ's resurrection is what *guarantees* this glorious outcome.[2]

14. Keeping your place in 1 Corinthians, take a few minutes to read Romans 8:18-30. Use the following space to write down insights or things that deepen your understanding of what we have just studied in both Hebrews and 1 Corinthians.

---

2. Bruce Winter, *1 Corinthians*, ed. D. A Carson et al., *New Bible Commentary: 21st Century Edition* (Downers Grove, IL: InterVarsity Press, 2010), page 1184.

"Creation groans; we groan; and the Spirit groans. Creation groans because it is subject to frustration. We groan because we feel the brokenness of the world in our lives, often in our own bodies. God is not frustrated, nor is he broken; but through the Spirit, he feels our pain with us. Every groan we utter is echoed by the Spirit. … Your groan is taken up by the Spirit and presented to the Father in a form that matches the Father's purpose of making you like his Son. As a result, 'in all things God works for the good of those who love him'."[3] —Tim Chester

> "YOUR GROAN IS TAKEN UP BY THE SPIRIT AND PRESENTED TO THE FATHER IN A FORM THAT MATCHES THE FATHER'S PURPOSE OF MAKING YOU LIKE HIS SON."
> —TIM CHESTER

15. What is the purpose to which those who love God are called?

16. What is the good that God promises to those who love Him and are called according to His purpose?

In all of this—the glorification of Christ and the glory that we get to experience—it is vital to keep in mind the end goal of both Christ's work and of our being made like Him: *the glory of God.*

15. Turn back to 1 Corinthians 15 and finish verse 28 below:

> *"When all things are subjected to him,*
> *then the Son himself will also be subjected*
> *to him who put all things in subjection under him,*
> *_____."*
>
> *(1 Corinthians 15:28, ESV)*

THE END GOAL OF BOTH CHRIST'S WORK AND OF OUR BEING MADE LIKE HIM IS <u>THE GLORY OF GOD</u>.

---

3. Tim Chester, *Enjoying God*, (Epsom, United Kingdom: The Good Book Company, 2022), pages 126-127. Used by kind permission.

APPLY:

1. What did today's reading teach you about God *(any member of the Trinity)* **and His character?**

2. How do the things you've learned today change your heart?

- How do these truths shape or change your view of God?
- Has today's Scripture convicted you of any sin or wrong beliefs that you need to confess?
- Has the Holy Spirit revealed any changes that you need to make in your thoughts, beliefs, or behavior in order to walk in this truth?

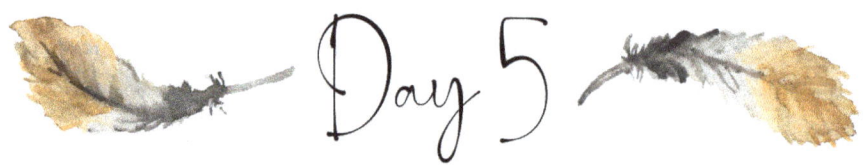

Day 5

READ: PSALM 102:18-28

We are really coming full-circle, having begun our study with this psalm and now ending with it as well. It is powerful to remember that through all of the things Christ did and that were done to Him, He remains our unchangeable Savior and our eternal Creator.

1. What purpose is given in verse 18 for keeping record of these things?

2. What things has the Lord done for His people (vv. 19-20) and why (vv. 21-22)?

HE
REMAINS
OUR
UNCHANGEABLE
SAVIOR

3. How do these verses give us a picture of what Christ *has done* through the gospel?

4. In what way do verses 21-22 reflect the *future* kingdom of God? Look up Revelation 5:9-10 if you need help with your answer.

5. In a moment we will review Hebrews 1:10-12, which quotes this psalm in reference to Christ. For now, read through Psalm 102:25-27 again and use the following chart to list everything that is said about Him.

VERSE	TRUTHS ABOUT CHRIST

READ: HEBREWS 1:10-12

We spent quite a bit of time digging into this passage on the first day of our study, so this is simply a review to remind us specifically of the divinity of Jesus Christ. The writer of Psalm 102 seems to be speaking to and of God the Father, yet the writer of Hebrews expands our understanding, pointing us to the truth that Jesus is God. He and the Father are *one* (John 10:30; 17:21-22).

READ: REVELATION 1:4-8

6. What phrase is repeated in verses 4 and 8?

7. Read the passage again carefully and note which member of the Trinity each of these repeated phrases is referring to:

- **Verse 4:** _____

(The first word of verse 5 should give you a hint if you're not sure.)

- **Verse 8:** _____

(If you need help, compare Jesus' words in Revelation 22:13.)

This is yet another reminder that though the Trinity is made up of three distinct Persons, they are all One God!

8. What names does John give Jesus in verse 5?

- *The _____ Witness*
- *The _____ of the _____*
- *The _____ of _____ on Earth*

Merriam-Webster defines a witness as, "one asked to be present at a transaction so as to be able to testify to its having taken place."[1] As our Faithful Witness, Jesus stands before the Father, faithfully testifying to the fact that our debt of sin has been paid in full!

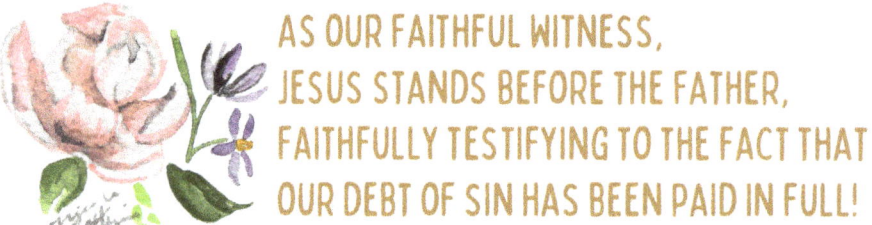

AS OUR FAITHFUL WITNESS,
JESUS STANDS BEFORE THE FATHER,
FAITHFULLY TESTIFYING TO THE FACT THAT
OUR DEBT OF SIN HAS BEEN PAID IN FULL!

If you'll recall from earlier in our study, we learned that the name "firstborn from the dead" carries the idea that Jesus is the founder and initiator of the new life God gives believers through His victory over sin and death. By His resurrection Jesus assumed first place in God's kingdom and opened the door for all believers to follow Him in resurrection. *(Refer back to day 4 of week 1 to take a closer look at this.)*

The title, "Ruler of Kings on Earth," points to Christ's supremacy over the hostile rulers of this world, "whose opposition cannot prevent the victory of His kingdom."[2] Regardless of how things appear, we can *know* that Christ's victory is sure. God's kingdom *will* reign victoriously!

---

1. Merriam-Webster.com Dictionary, s.v. "witness," accessed July 24, 2023, https://www.merriam-webster.com/dictionary/witness.

2. George R. Beasley-Murray, *Revelation*, ed. D. A Carson et al., *New Bible Commentary: 21st Century Edition* (Downers Grove, IL: InterVarsity Press, 2010), page 1425.

9. What do verses 5-6 say Christ does or has done for us?

10. Fill in the following blanks to finish verse 6:

"...to him be _____ and _____ forever and ever. Amen."
(Revelation 1:6b, ESV)

11. What does verse 7 tell us Christ will do?

12. What will people do in response (v. 7b)?

13. What causes this response in those who see Christ upon His return? *(Notice the specific groups of people named in this verse.)*

14. What names are given to Jesus in verse 8?

- _____
- _____
- _____

15. What is meant by the title, "Alpha and Omega"?

16. How does verse 8 specifically show Christ's eternality? Consider what we have learned from Psalm 102:25-27 as you answer.

17. How does the eternal and unchanging nature of Jesus impact the things He has done and will do?

One commentator says that by calling Himself "Alpha and Omega," Jesus is saying, "I am A to Z—the beginning and the end of history and Lord of all that lies between."[3] Even when worldly powers oppose His will and appear to be gaining ground, we can be sure that the Lord maintains perfect control. When you find yourself groaning with Creation, know that you can trust His promise to return, destroying death as the final enemy and making all things new. Because of this, we can "be steadfast, immovable, always abounding in the work of the Lord," *knowing* that in Christ our labor is not in vain (1 Corinthians 15:58)!

> "HE WHO TESTIFIES TO THESE THINGS SAYS,
> 'SURELY I AM COMING SOON.'
> AMEN. COME, LORD JESUS!"
> (REVELATION 22:20)

18. What work do you need to be steadfast in today? How does Christ's victory over sin encourage you in that work?

APPLY:

1. What did today's reading teach you about God *(any member of the Trinity)* **and His character?**

2. How do the things you've learned today change your heart?

- How do these truths shape or change your view of God?
- Has today's Scripture convicted you of any sin or wrong beliefs that you need to confess?
- Has the Holy Spirit revealed any changes that you need to make in your thoughts, beliefs, or behavior in order to walk in this truth?

---

3. George R. Beasley-Murray, *Revelation*, ed. D. A Carson et al., *New Bible Commentary: 21st Century Edition* (Downers Grove, IL: InterVarsity Press, 2010), page 1426.

Conclusion

What a journey it has been. What's next for you, friend? You've completed this study, but your work as a student of God's Word is not nearly finished. I encourage you to keep going! Choose a book of the Bible to study, and invite a friend to join you if you want someone to discuss it with and to hold you accountable to spending time with the Lord.

I hope that you can utilize some of the tools you gained through this study to build your confidence to begin studying the Bible on your own. You will never regret time and effort spent seeking to know the Lord through His Word! Bible study is not easy, but it is *always* worth it.

On the following page, I've compiled a list some of my favorite Bible study resources, along with a short description of each to help you know which ones might be most useful to you. However, I never want you to feel like you have to buy anything in order to study God's Word! These are simply tools that have greatly aided me in my own understanding. I am praying for you as you continue growing in your Bible study skills and especially in your knowledge of our Lord!

All for the glory of God,

Traci Mae

THE GRACE OF
THE LORD JESUS
BE WITH ALL.
AMEN.
REVELATION 22:21

BLUE LETTER BIBLE (phone app or <u>blueletterbible.org</u>)

Free access to Strong's Concordance as well as countless commentaries, sermon outlines, and other study tools.

BOOK OVERVIEWS

There are several options available, and each has its own unique advantages. Book overviews are helpful in understanding genres, authorship, themes, and unique aspects of each book of the Bible. **Two of my favorites are the *Bible Study Guide* from Chasing Sacred and *Book by Book* from The Bible Study Schoolhouse.**

IVP BIBLE BACKGROUND COMMENTARY

These are incredibly helpful during the observation stage of study, and one of the first resources I reach for in my own study! They provide historical and cultural information for the time periods in which each book/passage of the Bible was written! There is one volume each for the Old and New Testaments.

BIBLE DICTIONARY

There are of course too many Bible dictionary options available to list, but **my personal favorite is the *Holman Illustrated Bible Dictionary*.** It is written very accessibly and is full of helpful illustrations and photos!

COLOR-CODING SYSTEM

This is not everyone's cup of tea, but I find it immensely helpful to use a color-coding system to draw out insights regarding structure, repeated words, and other aspects of the text. For this, my top recommendation is of course what has become known as *The Bookmark* within our church family—**available as a free printable at <u>everydayberean.com</u>, or you can purchase physical bookmarks at <u>everydayberean.etsy.com</u> if you don't have a way to print them.**

COLORED PENS/PENCILS/HIGHLIGHTERS

Whether you use a color-coding system or not, it can be helpful to have a way to mark things that stand out to you. Find all of my favorite Bible-safe pens and highlighters at <u>everydayberean.com</u>!

SCRIPTURE JOURNALS

These are available in both ESV and CSB, typically printed in one journal per book of the Bible (some of the smaller books are combined). If you don't want to fill up your nice Bible with notations, questions, etc., this resource is for you! Scripture journals are simply the text of the Scriptures printed with extra margin and spacing between lines, alongside full blank pages. These are fantastic if you're an avid note-taker like me!

Find more Bible study recommendations and resources at <u>everydayberean.com</u>!

VISIT **EVERYDAYBEREAN.ETSY.COM** FOR PRINTS
FEATURING QUOTES FROM THE STUDY, COORDINATING
DRINKWARE, STATIONERY, APPAREL, AND MORE!

SCAN TO SHOP
ALL EVERYDAY
BEREAN
PRODUCTS!

PURCHASE PROFESSIONAL PRINTS OF EACH WEEK'S
FEATURED VERSE (ORIGINAL PAINTINGS BY NICOLE
RETHMEIER) AT **NOUVELLEMERE.ETSY.COM**!

SCAN TO
BROWSE ALL OF
NICOLE'S ART!